BECOMING AN ORACLE PROOF GOD HAS A SENSE OF HUMOR

True story of my face to face chat with God, Himself

GOD'S ORACLE

The events and conversations in this book have been set down to the best of the author's ability, although some names and details have been changed to protect the privacy of individuals.

Second paperback edition November 2019

Book design by God's Oracle

ISBN 978-0-578-60488-6 (paperback)

www.authorgodsoracle.com

DEDICATION

This book is dedicated to my amazing and beautiful daughters, loving husband and my dearest Father in heaven! Each of whom have always supported my crazy, unconditionally.

CONTENTS

ACKNOWLEDGMENTS

I would like to acknowledge God for His unconditional love and trust in me. He is truly the author of this amazing and life changing book. I would also like to give my deepest gratitude to my dear friend Linda for always believing without seeing.

PROLOGUE

July 5, 2018

"Do you accept this my child?" God said to me, while sitting on the edge of my bed and watching me intently with those heavenly blue eyes. I looked at my husband, Ian, hoping for some guidance. If I said yes, it would change Ian's entire existence, just as it would mine.

Ian was looking between father and I as if he were watching a tennis match and holding his breath while waiting for my answer. *Okay*, I think to myself, *I am obviously on my own with this decision.*

You may think that this is a simple question and should have an obvious answer. It is God after all and He had spent the last three hours telling Ian and me, in detail, the job he was requesting I do for Him. God, Himself, was asking me to work directly for Him and not in the way that you might imagine.

God was NOT expecting me to minister, spread His word, start a new church or a new religion. He did not even request for me to convince people to believe in Him. Those jobs would have a simple answer. But alas, No. God had something entirely different in mind for me.

It's not like I could tell God that I was hoping to work on my tan that summer or that starting a new job right now would unquestionably put me behind on holiday shopping.

This was **God**, and He wanted an answer. **Right now**.

I did not know the 'chatting with God while he sat on the edge of your bed' etiquette. We didn't cover that in Sunday School, I'm sure of it. That would be beneficial knowledge to have today.

I didn't want to be disrespectful, but I needed some clarification on a few points. Vital questions that would surely help with this impossible decision.

Questions like would this be a part-time or full-time gig? Is this a work from home thing or would I need to travel? How much travel? Would this position be considered management level or more of an entry level situation?

More importantly, Ian wouldn't be my boss, right? Ian being my boss could be a deal breaker.

Wait, will I have to quit smoking? What about cussing and tattoos? Is that going to be problem? Ian drinks beer. You know we are only human right?

God's promise of peace, love and joy with NO fear every

day for the rest of our human lives was a pretty good selling point. How could I say no to my Father in Heaven who had given me everything?

So, with a nod, I humbly said, "Yes Father, I accept."

CHAPTER ONE

July 5, 2018

The morning began normally enough for my husband, Ian, and me. We were discussing our plans for the day while lying in bed facing one another.

We had learned early on when our two beautiful girls were little, that this time alone would be the only time in the day we would have each other's full attention with no distractions. This also allowed us to synchronize our watches for the day's events.

Although both girls were now adults, it had become a habit over the last 23 years. It was my favorite part of my day; Ian is beautiful to look at.

I first laid eyes on my handsome husband when I was 24 years old while walking into a country western bar with my friend Sarah. As we strolled in, I saw the most exceptional sight.

He was a tall, tan, exceptionally good-looking guy with the most amazing blue eyes. He had a strong jawline and muscular build, just my type.

I turned to Sarah to make sure she was seeing this vision of perfection before us. I stood there, pleading with my eyes for her just know what I was thinking. I'm sure that I looked like a fish out of water, moving my lips with no sound coming out.

I was having a hard time forming any words, and that was not normally a problem for me. Most of the time, I struggled with too many words forming. Then the words would jump out of my mouth like a bat out of hell, racing to the ears of every being within hearing distance.

Sarah tried to nudge me toward the bar for a drink and the cute bartender she always flirted with. But I could not move. I froze in place just staring at her, then back at the divine being disguised as a man, just ten feet away.

"I will marry him" I said to Sarah, pointing to the mortal god standing mere feet from us.

"He is hot!" Sarah said, checking out the guy's rear. She was staring as if chocolate cake and teenage dreams made up the ingredients of his backside.

"No, Sarah. You don't understand. I know I have never met him, but I know him. That is my soulmate." I tried to explain to Sarah. It was hard to articulate my words due to the sensation of complete astonishment washing over me.

Sarah gave me her best 'there you go again with your intuition thing' look and walked to the bar to get a drink and a wink from her favorite bartender.

I have been 'different' my whole life and often treated cruelly by others because of those differences, especially by my family when I was a child.

I have always had a strong intuition and could see and hear things that other people could not. Often, when meeting people for the first time, I automatically knew personal experiences from their lives without being told.

Most of the time, it would be an experience that they had told no one. Not that I would blurt out their private information, but it always seemed to come to light at some point.

This always freaked people out.

My mother had warned me at a very young age that I could not tell people about these thoughts that randomly came to me, because the doctors would lock me up in the looney bin and experiment on me with needles. Needles and my mother were my biggest fears at four years old.

To be fair to my mother, she had just introduced me to her new boss. My initial question for this wise man would be the beginning of an event that would shape my entire childhood and path on this earth.

"Does my daddy know that you kiss my mommy when you are by yourselves?" I asked with the innocence of my young age. "I didn't know you could have a boyfriend and a husband."

I was a little kid, and I was curious. He was the boss of the joint; he should know all the answers. Or at least know where to find them.

He looked at my mom in complete disbelief that she had told her 4-year-old daughter that she was having an affair with her boss. He knew there was no way that I could have seen them together. They were way too careful; My daddy was a police officer.

My mother silently shook her head with a look on her face that said, "I said nothing".

They both seemed to have trouble using their big boy and big girl words. So, being a thoughtful child, I continued with another question. Just to get the ball rolling again.

"Does your wife know that my mommy is your girlfriend?"
I said in my most polite manner. I knew all too well that my
mother disciplined impolite children harshly.

Apparently, he was a nice boss. Not only did he give my
mommy kisses when they were alone, but he also let her have the
rest of the day off.

My mommy and daddy had a big fight that day. I guess my
daddy did NOT know that my mommy had a boyfriend, and daddy
was very mad. I think Mommy told daddy about her
boyfriend/boss that day, so I didn't ruin the surprise.

My daddy moved out that day. He told my mommy he had
rights because he was my daddy. He told her he would never stop
fighting for custody of me. So, mommy took his right to be my
daddy away.

Mommy always told daddy not to play games with her
because mommy always wins.

Mommy responded to daddy's demands to see me with a
piece of paper the judge called a restraining order. It said my daddy
had been hitting mommy and me.

Mommy told a policeman that my daddy said he would take
me with him and not bring me back. Mommy said that we were in

fear of our lives. I didn't tell the policeman mommy was lying. She had already shown me what would happen if I told.

My daddy was a police officer and spanking your wife and child would get you in trouble. Mommy said that her boss/boyfriend had lots of money and friends where we lived, and he would fix my daddy. Daddy's boss said daddy couldn't be a policeman anymore. I don't think daddy was broke before he met my mommy.

I didn't see my daddy again for a long time. But the day we went to see the judge again, my daddy was there. He looked so sad and tired, but he gave me a big smile! The policeman let me hug him, but just one time. I told my daddy I would go to McDonald's with him because his tummy was too skinny.

When the judge asked me if my daddy had been hitting me when he lived in our house, I looked right at that silly judge.

"No! My daddy would never hurt me! I'm his little princess!" I told that judge. I looked up and saw my daddy give me a big smile and he didn't look so sad anymore.

Mommy told the judge I was just scared of what my daddy would do to us if I told the judge the truth. I looked at mommy to say that was not true, but I saw her 'wait until we get home look' she had on her face.

I was so scared that I did not talk anymore to that judge, no matter how hard he tried to make me. I think I made the judge mad because he said I couldn't hug my daddy anymore or go to McDonald's with him.

A nice policeman was taking me to the bathroom and asked me to tell him the truth about my daddy. He promised he would not tell mommy anything, so I told him the truth.

The nice policeman told me he had a big surprise for me, but I could tell no one because he would get in big trouble. I promised I wouldn't tell and gave him a pinky swear like my daddy had taught me. You can't break a pinky swear.

He took me into a little room and my daddy was there! My daddy and I both cried a lot. Daddy told me to be a good girl and to hide in my closet when mommy gets mad. My daddy said that he loved his little princess SO much and told me NEVER to forget.

The nice policeman told daddy I had to go back to my mommy. I think they were friends because my daddy hugged him and gave the policeman a bunch of dollars. I'm not supposed to tell about that either though.

Mommy had already given me a big spanking the day my daddy moved out. She said that I had ruined everything with my big mouth.

Mommy said that if she would have known she had given birth to a freak, she would have left me at the hospital.

"I wish I would have been here when you tried to drown her when she was six months old." mommy said to my big brother while pointing at me. "I wouldn't have stopped you, that's for sure!"

That day with the judge was very confusing to my young mind. My dad had never laid a hand on me or my mom. It was my mother that had been beating me. And my dad. We were both terrified of her.

Looking back as I write this, I believe my father never spoke of the abuse we received because he was a member of law enforcement and embarrassed. Feeling that if he could not protect himself or his little girl, how could he protect his community? I also believe that my father truly loved my mother and held on to hope that it would get better.

Since my father was now unemployed, a disgraced police officer and broke, it was easy for my mother to have his parental rights terminated and to get a speedy divorce. She married her boss nine days after his divorce was final.

My older brother and I did not have the same father, and I don't remember my brother's biological father being in the picture as I was the youngest. Within a year of my mother's union with her boss, I had a new last name. Her new husband had adopted me and my older brother.

I never saw my dad again.

The story my mother recounted to me anytime I cried for my father was that he never wanted children, and that he never believed I was his child. She told me he had threatened her with divorce if she did not find somewhere else for me to live. My mother said she told him she would not send me away, so he left. My mother was very unrelenting in reminding me of the sacrifice she made, giving up her beloved husband, so I would not have to go into foster care like my father wanted.

It is amazing what they can condition you to believe in a lifetime. Even when you saw the truth with your own eyes.

My 4-year-old brain could not reconcile the loving father who called me his princess with the man my mom was describing. I can remember sobbing so many times uncontrollably out of hurt and confusion. I was quickly reminded that my mother would not stand for crying children.

My mother would tell me to be grateful for my "new" daddy. She would remind me to be a good girl because my old daddy was not coming back.

Sometimes I would slip and forget to recount the 'perfect life' fairytale my mother always recounted regarding how she met my adoptive father. My mother, older sister, and older brother would give their best embarrassed but fake loving smile while looking at me and shaking their head.

They would then explain that I was mentally ill or just a liar, whichever description fit their aim for that day the best. My family was not picky about whom they shared my disabilities with, nor whether it transpired quietly or privately.

I learned quickly that no one was exempt from my family's campaign to protect the public from me. Not even my teachers, employers, friends, or boyfriends. If I did not follow the script they had told me to use, my family would make sure I would regret it.

So, I stopped trying to defend myself against my families lies with facts; it would only result in pain or humiliation. A hot iron to a small child's hand makes a lifelong impression. No pun intended.

When things got unbearable at age ten, I asked my mother if I could find my dad and live with him. I offered to do all the work to find him and pay my way to get to him with my money. She refused to even tell me my father's name.

Being her thoughtful self, she reminded me again that he left because he didn't want me, and she was sure that he had not changed his mind. She added some new details this time though. My mother stated that my father was a horrible man that had been beating her and cheating on her. I felt guilty bringing up such awful memories of her past.

I did finally find my father in 2014. He had passed away ten years earlier in 2004. He had been living only two hours away from me for several years.

When I inquired about siblings, they told me that although my father had married again; he did not have another biological child. He also had never spoken of me or my mother to anyone I could find.

The fact he never spoke of me was very painful at first. Were the stories my mother told me about my dad leaving because he didn't want me true? I would find the truth in a photo album that had belonged to my father's mother, my grandmother.

This wonderful book displayed pages and pages of pictures of me with my dad. He was holding me and smiling in every picture. I saw him looking at me lovingly like I had seen Ian do a million times with our girls over the years.

I realized in that moment that my dad had loved me very much. Whatever had really happened between my mother and him was obviously too painful for him to talk about.

I was unaware yet that my mother had taken me from him in such a cruel way. I would not find the legal documents that led me to the truth of what my mother had done to my father and me for another five years after finding those pictures. Just a few short weeks before beginning to write this book.

So much pain and suffering had begun with that one random event when I was 4 years old. I had learned the hard way to keep my abilities to myself until I met Sarah.

Sarah was the first person I had trusted enough to tell about my curse since I was a child. She was not like other people I had encountered in my youth. She was open-minded and picked up on the fact that I was unique quickly and it fascinated her instead of causing her to run away.

She helped me to see how special I am, not an embarrassment or damaged. We meet in high school and over the years of our friendship, Sarah has seen so much evidence of what I can do to help other people. Even with no clear explanation of how, she loves me anyway.

Sarah had come to my defense frequently with family, friends, and even strangers. Those events would normally be someone's ignorance or fear overcoming their ability to accept things they did not understand or believe in. Sarah seemed to take it personally when people would be unkind to me because of my capabilities. She did not care who you were; you would get an ear full.

Sarah wasn't afraid of anyone, not even my mother, which was a complete wonder to me. Everyone was afraid of my mother.

"I can't wait to see all of their faces when you show the world who you really are. You will change this world for the good." Sarah would tell me while wiping my tears. I have wondered many times over the last year if Sarah was an angel sent from heaven to prepare me for this space in time.

But I digress, let's get back to the hot dude.

I quickly realized that this god among men was with a large group of people, and I did not have the courage to approach him that night. I knew that God would send him my way again when the time was right. This was a little preview to wet my whistle, I think.

I could not have imagined how fast that reunion with my soulmate would be or just how hilarious God's sense of humor was. Fast forward to the following Thursday.

Earlier in the week, I had gone out on a date with a guy we will call Jeremy. Don't judge please. I didn't know how long it would be before Father would send my demigod back on to my path again so I figured I should stay busy. That way I would stay out of trouble.

Anyway, Jeremy was a jerk! The entire night he talked about himself, and NOTHING else. At this point in my life, my early 20s, I believed the conversation should always be about me. It was obvious for both of us that this would not be any kind of love connection, not even a like connection.

A few days after this disastrous date, I received an odd phone call at work. This was the early 1990s, and we did not have cellphones, so it was common for people to contact each other at work. So, it was not surprising when the receptionist told me I had a call on the main line.

When I picked up the phone, a very pleasant male voice said, "Hi! I am Jeremy's brother; you went out with him earlier this week. What are you doing Saturday night?"

"Whoa, Whoa. I think you may have the wrong girl dude. I don't date brothers." I said, annoyed and offended.

"No, no. I'm sorry. Let me start again. I am Jeremy's brother. Saturday is Jeremy's birthday and I am throwing a surprise party for him on that day." the male voice said embarrassed. "I got your number out of his phone book. I was hoping you could help me get him to the party."

You have got to be kidding me. Jeremy the 'talk about nothing but himself all night' guy? I don't think so! I would rather spend my Saturday night shaving a porcupine.

But then, there it was. That inner voice, that intuition, my gift, that told me to say yes. Telling me something very important would happen that night, and I needed to be there.

I really did not want to go. I started thinking of where I could find a porcupine to shave on such short notice. How hard could it be to find a porcupine living in Texas?

"Ok, where and what time?" I heard myself say. What? What in Hades did I just say? I am truly losing it! I screamed in my head.

The male voice then gave me the details of my mission and hung up before I could get his name or a contact number. God had left me no way out of this event.

Against my better judgment, I called Jeremy and asked him if I could take him to dinner for his birthday. He said yes, making sure I knew of the sacrifice he was making in allowing me to take him to dinner. It was his birthday and it would disappoint thousands of his adoring fans.

What a lucky girl I was to pay for his dinner that night. Shoot me now, please, continued to replay in my mind. I reminded myself to call that farmer back about borrowing his porcupine Saturday night.

Saturday night arrived, and I picked Jeremy up for our 'date'. My plan was to take him to the appointed place at the appointed time and then run away, far away. When we walked into the agreed upon location, I stopped dead in my tracks.

There, across the room, was that guy, the demigod! That blue-eyed angel of man that would be my husband, my eternal mate, and he was looking right at me.

I stood there frozen like a statue in my jean shorts and Mickey Mouse sweatshirt, chastising myself for not taking more time on hair, make-up and outfit.

I had assumed that neither Jeremy nor the porcupine would care about my appearance, never imagining that my future husband would lay eyes upon me that night.

As I stood there, completely in shock, my future spouse walks towards me, still staring directly into my eyes.

I look around anxiously, thinking to myself, how am I going to shove Jeremy to the ground, step on his head to keep him quiet without this dream in jeans thinking I am with someone? I had completely forgotten about the porcupine at this point.

I look around trying to think of something fast because my eternal happiness depends on what I do next. As I look back toward the man of my dreams, I realize it was too late. He is now only a few steps away, and he is walking straight for me.

I scanned the room one more time, just in case a miracle is materializing, but see nothing obvious. Resigned to my fate, I look up into the face of my future and realize he is not looking at me at all.

He is looking lovingly at... Jeremy? Man, did I read this dude wrong I thought in complete shock.

"Happy birthday, little brother." My now husband, Ian says to Jeremy.

You... have... got... to... be... kidding... me! This will be awkward at family holidays. I look up at the Heavens and God and silently say why do you hate me? What have I ever done to you?

It all worked out though because God had a plan.

Jeremy in true jerk fashion called another girl to join him at the party as his date. Ian, my knight in shining armor, came to my rescue, and we have been together ever since.

It was a little strained at first with Jeremy, but he turned out to be a good guy and married a wonderful woman. They also have three beautiful children together.

CHAPTER TWO

July 5, 2018

"So… do you feel the need to leap up and dash to the grocery store to acquire any dairy products? But then not buy anything to bring home?" my husband jokingly asked.

It had been a whole month since the 'grocery store incident'. The day that I ran out of the house in my pajamas without brushing my hair or teeth, approach an innocent 64-year-old man in the grocery store, and ask him if I could put my thumb between his eyes. Come on, hasn't everyone done that at least once in their life?

Didn't that sweet little old man tell me thank you afterwards? Didn't that kind gentleman tell me through the tears he had been trying to heal that emotional trauma for over 60 years, and we healed it in 60 seconds? I feel Ian should respect this when attempting to hide judgement as a dad joke.

I know I should be more considerate of Ian's dad jokes. Ian is now at the age where it condemns him to only draw humor from his repertoire of dad jokes. But I am confident that he has hit his lifetime quota.

Thankfully, Ian still looked like the perfect vision I saw when I walked into that country western bar twenty-four years ago. The years had been very kind to Ian, minus the dad jokes.

I provide the love of my life with my best, you're so funny face. He smiled at me, knowing this face well. He fully knows that I am about to tell him exactly why he is wrong.

"Ian!" I said in my most firm teacher's voice. "As you may remember, that nice gentleman was thanking me and crying tears of joy. I gave him the courtesy of looking deep into his grateful and beautiful eyes before I quickly turned away and ran out of the grocery store sobbing."

Again, I'm sure everyone has done that at least once in their life!"

How could I have possibly known that my flight instinct would override my act like a normal human being instinct that day? When was my husband going to let this go?

Okay, in all honesty, I know how crazy the whole event sounds. But in my defense, the past few months had been a little strange. I was still trying to figure out if I was crazy or had a brain tumor. WebMD had said a brain tumor was a good possibility with the symptoms I was exhibiting.

I kept asking God for a sign that the events that had been happening over the last thirty days were real and not just a thousand random coincidences. I was trying to determine if I was hearing Father or if Ian had planted microphones all over the house to make me crazy.

Ian has always told me that when I turned fifty, he would trade me in for two twenty-fives. Fifty was only a few years off and now I was showing signs of being delusional. I begged Father to give me another sign.

In true God fashion, He would lovingly give me an event to show me that everything I was experiencing was extraordinarily real, and it was Him, not Ian, I was hearing.

I would be in complete awe for a space of time, then subsequently question said event. Eventually, I would convince myself that it was just a coincidence or mental illness.

Then, magically, it would happen again. I would ask Father once again for another sign that it was not just a brain tumor. Once more, Father would send me another unmistakable event to clarify to me I did not have a brain tumor.

Around and around we went.

What I didn't take into consideration at the time is that God has an eternity to play this game, along with infinite patience. I have a mortal body and a limited attention span. The odds were not in my favor.

What would you do? Would you blindly believe you were hearing God? Or would you go to the doctor three times a week for an entire month like I did?

The beginning of my internal struggle began on the evening of May 5, 2018. I was sitting on my bed painting my toenails while Ian was on his way to work.

I did not like it when Ian worked nights, so I tried to stay busy. I had spent so many nights sleeping alone during Ian's twenty years in the Army. I had hoped those nights were over when he had retired a few months earlier.

My youngest daughter, Jenae, was in her room doing homework or sleeping, like most high school students do on school nights.

And my mother was sleeping in her room downstairs.

Surprise! Plot twist! I bet you didn't see that coming!

I know you think that I am a saint for taking my mother in after the nightmare she made my childhood. Or maybe you are thinking it is more proof of my mental illness. It could have gone either way.

For clarification, our decision to bring my mother into our home was mostly because I did not remember the full truth of my childhood. Nor had I found the legal documents to prove my mother had manipulated everyone around her so expertly.

They had conditioned me since birth that I owed her for her selfless choice to allow me to remain in her home.

It was never a matter of my mother letting me live in her home. The issue was my mother's obsession with moving out in the middle of the night with a married man while I was asleep.

I was a junior in high school when my mother made her final middle of the night move out with no warning. I doubt it was her last, but it would be the last one that would complicate my life.

My mother had left with her current married boyfriend, but she was considerate enough to leave me a hundred dollars. I was grateful because they had taken every scrap of food and I did not get paid from my part-time after-school job for another two weeks.

Also, in my favor, my mother could not get a refund on the monthly rent for the trailer we were living in, so I still had a place to sleep until the end of the month. I had a whole ten days to figure something out.

How hard could it be for a sixteen-year-old in a new town to find a place to live on a part-time job?

I knew I would have to work full time now while I finished high school. Thankfully, in the 80s, child labor laws would not be an issue. Besides, it's not like this was the first time my mother had slipped away in the middle of the night.

Nope, this middle of the night move out was lucky number three in the last two and half years. The first time my mother did the whole gone girl act, I was fourteen.

I was just waking up for school one morning when my older sister walked into my room. She told me that our mother was dying of cancer.

My sister said that our mother had left in the middle of the night to move across the country for treatment with her current married boyfriend. My mother had told my sister that was the only treatment center that could treat the cancer my mother had.

The news of my mother dying was exceptionally heartbreaking since I had just lost father number two, barely two years earlier.

The first father had left because he knew I was a freak; my mother had readily advised me at age twelve. She had added the freak detail to her previous rendition of my father's absence, when I requested again to find him so I could unburden her with my presence.

My mother told me she was positive that my father would have nothing to do with me due to my freak status, therefore, not worth the time and effort to locate him.

I burst into tears with the new information that my father thought I was a freak like the rest of my family. I realized my father wanted a child; he just did not want me.

My second father, my mother's boss who had adopted me, had died of a heart attack when I was twelve, six months before I requested to live with my biological father.

Sitting with my sister and listening to the seriousness of my mother's diagnosis, I silently started to wonder if this was my fault. I had already caused my mother so much heartache and shame in my fourteen years on earth. Had I somehow caused her to get cancer too?

I didn't deserve to have her as my mother. I had been such an enormous burden on everyone in my family.

I begged God to allow me to give my life so that my mother could live. It would be six months until I finished the school year and could move there to care for her. I was grateful that she had someone to take care of her until then.

The married man that left town with my mother had walked away from all that he had built in his life to help save my mother's life. Maybe he could be the hero my mother seemed to need.

He had disappeared in the middle of the night with my mom, abandoning his job as a police officer and his family.

As it turned out, my mother did not need a hero. I would not need to give up my life so that my mother could live either!

She did not have cancer; she never had cancer! She did not even have a cold!

You may wonder if I am recounting a miracle to you right now. Wonder no more, my friend! The answer is NO, it was not miracle that my mother was cancer free.

It was instead an elaborate scheme that my mother had designed to get her married boyfriend to leave his wife and three small children.

My mother's hero had believed my mom when she said she was dying of cancer just like I had, without question. It did not take long for my mother's ball of lies to unravel.

When my mother would not allow her hero to go to the doctor with her, it hurt his feelings.

When she didn't bring home any prescription medications or vitamins from the doctor, he began to get suspicious.

When my mother showed no signs of getting sick and no sign of side effects from the poison the cancer treatment required her to ingest, he investigated.

He had been a police officer for ten years. I'm sure it didn't take long for a trained investigator to find the truth.

My mother's hero gave me the news of her deception shortly after arriving to live with them. The man who had abandoned his family and job to save my mother's life.

The hero angrily recounted the reality of my mother's health as he was packing his truck to bursting. He took everything he had painstakingly gained over the last six months with him.

The hero looked me directly in the eyes while saying that my mother had taken enough from him. *Welcome to my world,* I thought to myself.

My mother's hero briefed me on his very thorough investigation, which included pictures, written statements from the cancer center medical staff and my mother's medical records.

It was not shocking that my mother had lied, I had expected it. The shocking news to me was that he had not expected my mother to lie.

The content of the evidence didn't really interest me. I didn't need proof that my mother would lie to get what she wanted. I was however, impressed with his attention to detail and hard work.

When I told him what a great job he did getting to the truth, he began a whole new rant.

He explained heatedly to me how hard it is to get a job when you are an ex-cop that disappeared in the middle of the night with a woman.

He added that it was impossible to get a job if that woman was not your wife.

I knew he was looking for sympathy from me, but I was not the one to give it to him. I had very strong feelings regarding a father leaving a child, even back then.

To be fair, I barely knew this guy, but he had always been nice to me. He had even stood up to my mom on my behalf a time or two.

This had given me hope for the future during my six-month imprisonment living alone with my sister and brother after my mom had left the state for her bogus cancer treatment.

My mother's hero told me he would go back to our hometown and beg his wife to forgive him, and then beg his boss to give him his job back. He said he had learned his lesson and wanted to be the best husband and father he could be for his family.

Good for you dude, I sincerely said in my head as I watched him drive away.

When I saw his taillights go around the corner, I realized that I was sad to see him go. The hero and I had something in common. We had both learned from the master, my mother, that 'no good deed goes unpunished'.

As I said previously, when my mother left for her cancer treatment, it left me with my siblings.

It was a long six months and our house was under a new regime. The new tyrant, my sister, made sure I knew of the level of burden I was now placing on her.

My sister's burden of caring for me became so great that it inspired her to recruit my brother to lighten her duty by taking over the physical discipline when I would not comply with their demands, immediately, when ordered.

To be honest, the physical discipline wasn't that bad. During the six months sentenced to live with my siblings, my brother was normally too drunk or stoned to remember that my sister had ordered a beating for me.

Not to mention, I was excellent at making myself invisible.

My brother had done so much worse to me throughout my lifetime, so this was a cakewalk. He had tried to assassinate me several times over the years.

No, really… I'm not joking. My brother planned and attempted to murder me as a child on countless occasions.

My brother's first attempt to end my life was to drown me in the bathtub. I was six months old; he was three.

Over the years he would attempt to drown me five or six more times.

I became an excellent swimmer.

My brother's next brainstorm was a fatal fall from the top of our barn. Throwing me out of the hayloft or shoving me off the roof only seemed to frustrate him.

Although, it is possible that his frustration came from me always landing on piles of hay that were not there when he went into the barn.

I learned how to tuck and roll from high places without breaking bones like batman's stunt double.

My brother's next inspiration was a fatal horse-riding accident. Being a Sociopath, he did not understand the bond developed over time between horse and rider and I had ridden that horse a lot.

I became well versed in riding a bucking or rearing horse.

My brother learned that a horse's hoof to the groin, might rupture a testical.

But my favorite was the "accidental" shooting plot. This is where I could hone my hide or flight responses.

I fully know that the term is **fight** or flight response, but I wanted to live. So, fighting back was not an option.

I did, however, devise an escape plan that would become a lifelong mantra for me if being shot at.

1. Run.

2. Complete number one in a zigzag pattern.

3. Complete number one and two as fast as you can, at the same time.

Don't laugh. Believe it or not, it takes practice to master running as fast as you can in an effective zigzag pattern without getting hit with a bullet.

I also became excellent at hide and seek. I could hide in plain sight without moving for hours.

My brother may have been an exceptional liar and a manipulator, but thankfully NOT gifted in planning and executing assassination attempts.

I tried to tell my mother about my brother's attempts on my life many times. I finally accepted that it was a waste of time.

Whenever I tried to tell my mother what had transpired, my brother would come up with some alternate narrative where I was the villain.

My brother would enviably end his storyline with "You know how she lies mom" or "You know she has mental problems mom".

Her anger at being bothered with such trivial things as my attempted murder would inevitably become my fault. That would end with my perceived transgressions being dealt with harshly.

The burden of me living in the same house would normally come up during my punishment.

In our adult years, it became a frequent topic of conversation during any holiday dinner with my mother and siblings.

They would discuss each of my brother's failed plots to end my life and laugh uncontrollably. It was as if they were recounting attempts to end the existence of an old and mangy cat with nine lives instead of a terrified little girl trying to survive, never knowing where or when the next attack would be.

My beautiful daughter Jenae was my inspiration for ending the brutal holiday tradition of recounting my terror as a child. My mother and siblings were usually careful about having story time in front of Ian or my girls as they were very protective of me.

Ian and the girls knew of the abuse from my childhood, just not the severity of it. They had conditioned me over the years that only misery came when giving the details of my abuse. I feared Ian or the girls may suffer the backlash with me if I shared too much.

On this specific holiday dinner, my brother had too much to drink. He was feeling extra brave and just could not help himself.

He recounted one of my most horrific memories as a child. It had been my brother's most triumph moment because he could destroy something I had dared to love.

This event would teach me if I loved anything or anyone, I would subject them to live the same nightmare as I was. It removed all doubt that anyone would be safe coming into the horrendous existence that was my life.

I had several barbie dolls growing up and I loved them dearly. I would spend hours brushing their hair and playing tea party with them.

Susan was my favorite; she made the best tea. They were my friends and my escape when banished to my room when looking at me became unbearable for my mother and siblings.

On one of the worst days of my childhood, I had spent several hours in the basement building a fort for the ultimate tea party. I had Susan and the girls safely tucked away in my room, under my bed eagerly waiting for me to finish.

It was cold and smelled in the basement, but my brother feared the farthest room, so that was where I was safest. He believed it haunted, but I was more afraid of him than something I couldn't see.

In the late afternoon, I had gone upstairs to use the bathroom. Unfortunately, my brother was coming in from the outdoors at the same time.

I was instantly on high alert when I saw the pure evil smile on his face when he saw me.

I froze in the place like a deer in headlights because I knew what that look meant and it wasn't good. I was trying to process quickly if I could make it back down to the basement before he caught me, but my mind froze in fear just like my feet.

When I finally convinced my feet to move, my brother put his hands up as if to surrender.

"I will do nothing to you. I have a surprise for you." He said in that way that told me I needed to be cautious. "Come look out the window."

I was still trying to gauge the safest path. My mother and adoptive father would not be home for at least another two hours.

I know from experience the damage my brother could do in two hours if he could catch me. I was chastising my bladder when my brother took several steps back from the window.

"I will even stand way back here so you know I can't touch you." He said with that same sickening smile on his face.

I decided to just look and get it over with. He was far enough back that I could get away out the front door if I had to. I didn't have any shoes on, but I had been barefoot in snow before and it would be better than the alternative.

I cautiously approached the window while keeping my brother in clear view and an escape path in mind. What I saw when I looked out the window would haunt my dreams for the entirety of my lifetime.

There was a huge oak tree directly outside this specific window. I could see several objects hanging in the tree and scattered on the ground around the tree.

As I got closer to the window for a better look, I began to fight the need to vomit and in doing so urinated in my pants.

Hanging from the tree was the head of every one of my beloved barbies.

Their faces cut up and burned and hanging by their hair. I could also see now that the items I had noticed scattered on the ground under the tree were the mutilated bodies of each head.

He had not just popped their heads off but decapitated them with an axe now stuck in the tree.

Hanging directly in front and almost unrecognizable, I saw my beloved Susan. I knew it was Susan because of her beautiful long brown hair that I had brushed almost a million times to get her ready for our tea parties.

The grief that overcame me caused a pain in my chest I had never experienced in my short little lifetime.

It was so all-consuming that I did not even realize that my brother had step up beside me and was also looking out the window at his handy-work, smiling.

I didn't even startle when he leaned down and whispered right next to my ear, "I will put your head right next to Susan's." He then turned and walked away, laughing all the way to his bedroom.

Unfortunately for my brother, he had assumed I would go out and clean up the carnage. He disappeared into his room and did not come out again until my adoptive father was dragging him out all the while my mother was screaming at him to leave my brother alone.

My brother kept trying to tell our adoptive father that I had done it, not him. My mother was backing my brother up by agreeing that it was most likely me, not my brother that had done such an egregious act.

However, this would be the one time their habit of not seeing me would not work out in their favor.

My adoptive father had arrived home twenty minutes before my mother that day. The tree was right by the back door so he could not miss the horror.

When he came inside, he found me sitting on the floor next to the window and silently rocking back and forth and instantly knew what had happened.

My mother arrived just as my adoptive father was dragging my brother out of his bedroom. My adoptive father was an even tempered and calm man, so it was rare to see him angry much less raise his voice.

"Shut up!" My adoptive father screamed at both my mother and brother. They both went instantly still and stared at him. He then turned to my mother and looked at her with disgust.

"Did you even notice your daughter over there in a catatonic state? That child is in shock! She did not do this!" he continued to scream.

"How can you not see how sick this is? Our son needs help!" he said to my mother while removing his belt. He seemed to be astonished at her lack of concern for me.

Two things happened that day that gave me hope. My adoptive father held my brother responsible for his actions.

Next, he packed a bag for me and took me to his sister's house. She was a very sweet lady and took loving care of me for two weeks while I regained the ability to talk again.

My adoptive father brought me a new barbie every day of that two weeks and would try to coax me out of my mental prison.

I would never again touch or play with a barbie or any doll.

During my final holiday dinner with my mother and siblings, my brother proudly recounted the barbie story with glee in his voice. His rendition recounted that I had urinated in my pants but stopped just before the moment he told me he would add my head.

He has mastered over the years keeping the monster hidden. My brother's next action would be his undoing regarding my silence.

Jenae just had foot surgery a few days before and was resting on the couch with her foot propped up. She needed help to get around and was on some very heavy pain medication. She was in her own little world and playing on her phone during the most current retelling of my youth and did not pay much attention to the story.

"Do you have any barbies Jenae?" the monster asked while looking directly into my eyes with a challenge daring me to stop him. The festivities concluded shortly after.

Ian and I had kept our children far away from the monster their whole lives. The girls would stay with my mother occasionally, she was very loving and kind with them and they felt the same. Ian and I were very insistent that my mother not allow the monster over when our girls were there without us.

We had cautioned our girls from birth to never be alone with him if my mother went against our wishes. My mother did not honor our wishes frequently, but we prepared our girls.

Ian and I made sure they knew the truth so they could take measures to protect themselves until we could get to them.

Truth is how we do **NOT** continue the abusive patterns of the past.

The truth is, my brother added sexual assault to his homicide attempts when I was ten years old. It was my first day home after the barbie incident.

I immediately ran to my mother when I could get away from him. She had to believe me this time, the blood running down the inside of my legs had to be enough proof that it wasn't my fault this time.

"People don't talk about such things." my mother dispassionately stated. And that was that, conversation over.

After my adoptive father died when I was twelve, my brother never touched me sexually again. I have always wondered if it was my brother's fear that our adopted father was now watching him.

It didn't really matter to me why he stopped; I was just grateful the monster no longer came into my bed at night.

But even though the monster no longer slithered into my room in the dark, it would still take many years for me to feel safe sleeping at night.

A lot of time and an amazing man named Ian would help me remove my fear of the dark.

Ian showed me over the years what a loving relationship looked and felt like. He gave me the courage to be proud of my differences instead of being ashamed of them.

Ian finds it amazing and not disgusted by what I can do. Well, he began to find it amazing two years into our marriage since that is when I told him about it. I was trying to be a considerate and thoughtful wife by easing him into it.

Ian, my beautiful daughters and my many amazing friends had taught me over the years I was of worth. That my differences made me special and not a freak.

Even with the constant love and support of my husband, daughters, and friends, I still had to fight the overwhelming yearning to have my mother's love and approval.

A lifetime of conditioning made it difficult for me to comprehend that my mother could not give me something that she did not have access to within herself. I did not understand at the time that it literally had nothing to do with me. It had everything to do with how my mother saw herself.

My mother had been living with us since my most current stepfather had passed away. She was very ill at the time of his death and could not care for herself.

My siblings had made the decision that a nursing home was the best option, each of them expressing to Ian and me that their lives were not conducive to caring for a sick old woman.

The doctors had told Ian and me that my mother would not live for more than a month to six weeks. She had contracted sepsis, which was causing her organs to shut down. She was also in kidney failure.

I told Ian that we needed to move my mother into our house. I had hope that this could be my chance to earn my mother's love and respect. Maybe I could even make up for all the shame and hurt I had caused her over the years.

"It will only be a few months." I begged Ian.

That was two years ago, and she was now healthier than she had been in her previous ten years.

Welcome to my world!!!

(MESSAGE FROM THE AUTHOR)

I would like to thank you for staying with me through the difficult content of Chapters 1 and 2.

It is important for you to know my past trauma, so you can better understand the constant battle I was fighting at the beginning of this amazing journey. I had to find my truth so I could believe enough in **MYSELF** to accept God's job offer.

It is so vital for you to understand that no matter what your past has been; you have the God given right to decide what you want your future to be, with no judgement. Your past can only define you if you allow the fear you tolerated then, to be a part of what you are choosing to create for yourself now!

Let us get back to May 5, 2018 and the painting of my toenails. It is about to get very exciting!!!

CHAPTER THREE

I had no way to know that this night would be the beginning a journey that would cause the healing of my childhood trauma. This path would also permit me to live a life of complete peace, love and joy. And most of all, a life with NO fear.

So, I was finishing up my toenails while thinking about when Ian had been in the Army. We always seemed to struggle financially during those years. We could pay our bills but not much in the way of savings or extras.

Now Ian had a good job in the oil and gas industry. He was making more money in a week than he had made in a month while in the Army, and Ian was miserable. The new job required long hours, lots of travel and a monster for a supervisor.

I was sitting on the bed admiring the blue polish on my toes while thinking about Ian's new job and how unhappy he was. Suddenly, I heard a male voice right next to me on my bed.

"Ian needs to quit his job." the voice whispered.

The nearness of the voice startled me briefly because I believed no one was in the room with me. But a sense of peace suddenly came over me. I had heard that voice before, I knew I had.

I sat there on my bed, stunned and silent, waiting for something to happen. I got up and looked around to make sure Jenae was not pulling a prank on me.

I opened Jenae's door and she was sleeping, out cold. I went back into my room and sat on my bed still a little confused.

I jokingly said, "Was that you Father?"

I didn't feel fear, just curiosity. Surely God, Himself was not speaking to me while I was sitting on my bed painting my toenails.

"Ian needs to quit his job." The male voice said again, a little firmer.

Okay, that was unmistakable. That was GOD, talking to me!

It is hard to explain how I knew it was God. It was this amazing and intense feeling of peace, love and joy. When Father speaks to anyone this way, you just know inside of you it is Him. It is a sense of recognition that you feel all the way into your Divine Spirt.

God was talking to me.

Suddenly, I was self-conscious. Was I supposed to respond or was God just making a statement? Was He trying to start a dialog with me? Maybe I should say something. I didn't want God to think I was being rude and ignoring him.

"Ian doesn't have another one Father." I stated.

"Ian needs to quit his job." God said again in an insistent tone.

"Okay, but he doesn't have another one Father." I say again, more slowly and a little louder just in case Father didn't hear me clearly the first time.

I wasn't sure if age affects hearing in Heaven like it does on earth. Maybe I wasn't speaking loud enough for God to hear me.

"Ian needs to quit his job, my child." Father declared sternly.

I opened my mouth to repeat my newfound mantra of *he doesn't have another one* when Father gently added, "What are you willing to do to prove your faith, my child"?

Oh…He could hear me just fine. I sat silent for just a second while I marveled at God's skill to get me to see His point so quickly.

"I will do whatever you ask, Father." I whisper back as I reached for my cellphone.

Without even thinking what Ian would say about the event that had just played out, I called him. How would this be any crazier than the things Ian had witnessed as my husband over the past twenty-four years.

When Ian answered, I stated, "Hey babe, crazy thing just happened. God told me you need to quit your job."

I expected Ian to ask me if I hit my head causing me to hallucinate my exchange with God. I had at least expected him to pause for a moment to take in my words.

"I don't I have another one." Ian replied, not missing a beat and very matter of fact.

"That's what I said!" I exclaimed, excited that Ian and I saw this issue in the same light.

After a very brief discussion, Ian promised to pray about my shocking conversation with God on his way home. It was not until I hung up the phone, that I realized Ian had never questioned that it was God that spoke to me. He didn't even ask me if I was joking. Was he just playing along so I would not feel insane?

I went about my nightly chores, still amazed that Ian didn't think I was imagining things. I did not understand that our whole belief system of how to achieve happiness on earth was about to change forever.

The next morning Ian was in the kitchen when I got home from taking Jenae to school. He had just finished putting his lunch box and dirty dishes in the kitchen sink when he looked up and made eye contact with me.

"So, I prayed about quitting my job." Ian stated. "God told me to quit as soon as this contract ends."

I motioned for my husband to follow me up to our room where we could talk. I could not hear him over the theme song of my mother's TV show of the week she was watching at full volume.

I like Hawaii 5-0. I absolutely think Alex O'Loughlin who plays Steve McGarret is seriously hot. But when I can quote each word of every episode in all 7 seasons, it's time to move on to something new. Sorry Alex.

When we get upstairs, Ian starts his normal routine of taking off his dirty cloths and preparing to take a shower while I sit on our bed and play games on my phone.

This is Ian's time to unwind while he showers and prepares for bed. I think about how exhausted he looks.

Father, can you make Ian's new job not so physically taxing for him please. He is so drained all the time; I remember whispering in my head.

Ian was working 12-hour days, for thirteen days straight. After thirteen days he would get one day to rest then start the routine all over again.

It was hard work, but he never complained. He wanted his family to have everything he felt we had sacrificed while he was developing his career in the Army.

When Ian got out of the shower, I noticed the dark circles under his eyes. He looked like he was losing weight and his impossibly handsome face looked pale.

I silently agreed with Father that Ian needed to quit his job. It was slowly draining him of life. No amount of money would be worth his health and happiness.

His injuries from many war deployments and being in the military were quickly becoming more and more clear.

"So, what did Father say?" I casually asked Ian as he was dressing in his jammies. He laid down on the bed next to me and sighed.

"He told me I needed to quit my job." He flatly stated.

"I know that, but what else did he say?" I inquired.

"That is pretty much it. I asked Him if I should quit my job and He said yes." Ian said.

"That's it, nothing else?" I prodded.

Ian is a paraphraser. He will recount a two-hour conversation with an old friend that we haven't seen in ten years by saying, "They said we should get together soon."

Ian rolled his eyes and said, "I asked him when he wanted me to quit and He said to quit when the current contract is complete."

"Did he say what your next job might be?" I half-jokingly asked.

"Nope." He barely whispered.

I looked over and saw that Ian was already asleep. I kissed his forehead and moved to my side of the bed, so I didn't disturb him.

I trust you Father, I said in my head as I got up off the bed. I looked back at my one true love before leaving the room and gently shut the door.

Ian and I did not discuss what Father had instructed him to do over dinner that night. We did not know when this contract would wrap up and would discuss it further when that time came.

Father is not one to dally.

That night when Ian got to work, he called me so excited that I could feel the enthusiasm through the phone.

"When I got to work, they told me this would be our last shift! They said that the job is winding down and the night shift is being laid off!" Ian proclaimed excitedly.

Ian then told me that his employer had offered him another contract job that would pay $60,000 over the next five months.

That was a lot of money, but God had instructed Ian to quit when this contract was up. We had a decision to make.

"Let's talk about it tomorrow morning when I get home. We can both pray about it before then and compare what we hear." Ian declared. He had more excitement in his voice than I had heard in weeks, if not months.

When I got into bed, I wondered if I could start a conversation with God or if I should I wait until he contacted me. I am sure he must be busy running Heaven and earth, day and night, without a break. I didn't really want to bother Him, but I told Ian I would ask.

"Father, should Ian accept this new contract that is being offered?" I asked Father quietly.

I didn't want to interrupt God if he was in a meeting or something, but I was hoping He could fit me in for a few minutes. It was a lot of money and would allow us to improve our lives dramatically.

"Ian needs to quit his job, my child. He will need to do this in person to the man who hired him." God replied immediately. "I have something so much more for him and your family. Trust in me, my beautiful daughter for I trust in you. I will always bring everything you need to your doorstep."

Wow, that was a quick answer. He must have been between calls. He had spoken out loud to me again like He had the day before. I could hear him as if he was right next to me.

I sat amazed for a while. I was having a conversation with God! I could hear him like I could hear anyone else. It surprised me it seemed so natural to hear Father's voice, like we had been talking this way my entire life.

"I trust you Father. Thank you for all you have done for our family. I love you so very much." I said with such an intense feeling of peace, love and joy.

The peaceful feeling was so all consuming that I feared I would never fall asleep that night but sleeping would not be an issue. Immediately when I closed my eyes, I drifted off to sleep.

Peace, love and joy will do that to a girl.

The next day when Ian got home from work, I was still in bed. He approached the bed and sat down next to me.

"Father told me not to take the job." Ian said. Worry seemed to fill his voice.

"He told me the same thing." I said reassuringly. "He also said that He had something better for you!" I said excitedly.

I knew Ian would not like with my next words, so I quickly added, "But he also said that you would need to quit in person, to the man that hired you."

Ian looked at me like I had sprouted a horn and was threatening to poop rainbows like a unicorn. I love unicorns.

"Why do I have to go in person and quit? I can just call personnel and tell them not to put me on the job!" he shouted at me. Ian was not pleased with this new requirement, and it was obvious. Ian's shouting did not go over well with me.

After the horror I endured as a defenseless child, I had no intention of allowing anyone, not even my beloved husband, to scream at me for something I had no control over.

"DO NOT YELL AT ME! I'M JUST TELLING YOU WHAT GOD SAID TO ME!" I screamed back.

I know it is ridiculous to tell someone not to yell while doing it yourself. Unfortunately for Ian, I was feeling ridiculous right at that moment and a little saucy too.

"I'm sorry, your right. But why does he want me to go in person?" Ian says apologetically.

"I don't know why! You can ask Him yourself! It is not like God has hired me to work for him!" I said back in a snotty tone.

How uneducated I was back then. I would eventually have to eat those words. Well, not eat them actually, but you know what I mean.

"If I quit my job, we have no income except for my retirement from the Army. That will cover our rent, but what about everything else?" Ian stated, starting to calm down a bit.

We had been paying off bills with Ian's new higher paying job, but we had put nothing in savings. We had assumed that Ian would have this job until he was ready to retire from working. Now what? We had a teenager and a woman in her late seventies to care for.

Believe it or not, we came to the answer easily. We followed God's prompting.

Ian and I held hands and jump off that scary ledge called the unknown. Even though we could not see what was at the bottom of that dark hole, God could, and that was enough for us.

When Ian spoke to the man that had hired him, Ian was visibly nervous. There would be no going back once we did this.

Ian politely thanked the man who had given him the job for taking the time to speak to him. Then Ian went on the inform him he was quitting, effective immediately.

The man was rather shocked but assumed Ian had found another job. When Ian told him he did not have another job, the man, who had the best poker face in Texas, could not hide his shock. His mouth fell open briefly as he stared.

As Ian prepared to leave, the man reached out his hand and sincerely thanked him for coming in personally. He told Ian that he would always be welcome to come back and even offered to write him a recommendation letter.

This man had never shown Ian anything other than passing annoyance. He now seemed truly in awe and grateful that Ian had taken the time to come in and speak to him personally.

But it seemed his true astonishment was that we had made the choice to put Ian's health and our family's happiness ahead of the fear of not having enough money.

Ian called me that day while walking to his car after he had quit his job. I heard him shut his car door after getting in and let out a huge sigh.

"You realized this is the first time in 24 years that we have no income, right?" I asked Ian with affection and peace in my voice.

"I know." Ian said. "And I have never felt more peace in my life."

"Me too baby." I responded, "Me too." Ian and I both meant those words, heart and soul.

About six month later, Ian and I heard that the man who hired Ian, resigned from the company not long after Ian had. This man had worked there for many years but chose to start his own business. He would put his health and happiness ahead of the fear of not having enough money.

When I heard this news, I asked Father why he wanted Ian to quit in person that day.

"I wanted my son to remember the man he started out to be, and to see the man he had become." Father stated. "Over the years my son became obsessed with money and power. He had forgotten the peace that being an honest man brings."

Father was silent for a moment and then continued on by saying, "He saw his younger self in Ian that day. When Ian left, my son was overcome with the desire to have that peace within him again."

"Did it all work out the way you wanted?" I inquired from Father.

"It was only my desire to allow my son a reminder of what would bring true happiness to his life on earth. How he chooses to use his freewill is his decision. I promised I would never take freewill." Father replied. "But to answer your question, yes my child. It did indeed work out the way I had hoped for my son." He sweetly replied with a loving smile in his voice.

I sat there for a moment, admiring how Father can take one situation and affect millions of people in different ways. I made a vow right then and there. I would never play chess with God, never.

While waiting for Ian to drive home from the job he no longer had, I decided that I needed to prepare his resume. We had no savings so being off work for too long would put us in a bind.

I wasn't sure what job God wanted Ian to have but I knew it would be big. Ian had turned down a job paying $60,000 over five months. I was sure that the new one would pay at least that if not more.

I excitedly knelt at the foot of my bed and asked God for guidance on which Fortune 500 company I should send Ian's resume to.

I'm not positive, but I thought I heard Father laugh. Not just a little giggle, but a full-on belly laugh. Surely not, I must be mistaken.

Then I hear Father clear as day, just as before.

"Ian must rest until he knows who he wants to be." God informed me.

When Ian got home, I eagerly explained to him that God wants him to rest until he knows who he wants to be. Then, when he wakes up, he can tell me, and I could immediately send out his resume to the company and position.

We would have Ian a new job by mid-week at this rate!

Ian had gone straight from the military into the job he just quit with only enough time off to move and get settled. He deserved a nap.

"So, go lay down and take a nap. I'm thinking thirty to forty-five minutes should be plenty of time." I tell Ian with complete sincerity.

Ian gladly laid down to rest. It had been a stressful morning and he had not slept well expecting the meeting.

When Ian woke up 45 minutes later, he did NOT know who he wanted to be.

No, really. He did not know at all. I asked him, repeatedly. He had no clue! Maybe a good night's sleep will be the balance he needs to find himself.

A week of rest and video games for Ian went by without that AHA moment we were waiting for. That moment when Ian suddenly knows who he wants to be.

We had no money coming in but continued to have food going out of the cupboards and into my family's bellies. The electric and water companies still wanted money.

While I am not so patiently waiting on Ian to decide who he wants to be, I worry about feeding my family.

I asked Father what to do while we wait on Ian. He instructed me to go to our church for help. When I ask Father what to say, Father's response is simple. Say the truth.

How am I supposed to tell my church leader that God told Ian to quit his job? How am I supposed to tell this very conservative man of God that I can suddenly hear Father as if he is standing next to me?

I feel that this will not go well.

Our church leader gave me the "maybe you should see a doctor look" but agreed to help us with food until we got back on our feet.

He also told me he wanted to speak with Ian and I both on the upcoming Sunday. His assistant would call and let us know what time we would be meeting.

By the time I left the church leaders office, I was already doubting that I had spoken to God. I probably had a brain tumor.

Our church leader had explained to me I could not hear God because I was not a man. Second, I did not attend church every Sunday and I smoked cigarettes.

These transgressions would make it impossible to for little ole me to hear god.

Please understand. I never doubted that God was there or that Father was real. I have never doubted that other people had heard God speak to them. It was genuinely an issue of faith and worthiness in MYSELF.

But this man was right. What could be so special about me I could hear God like he was sitting next to me? I am not a divine being by any stretch of the imagination.

As a child, they told me I was a burden, worthless, and not wanted. Wouldn't that alone be proof that I was not worthy to hear God or be worthy of his time and energy?

I had made some major mistakes in my life. I know this to be true due to so many of my family, friends and fellow church members letting me know each time they observed my lack of perfection.

They would always make sure I knew of my transgressions, for my salvation.

By the sheer volume of the interest they seemed to show in my actions and their complete commitment to always make a comment to me or to others, I had sinned a lot.

Ian and I had lived together for a year before we got married and shared the same bed. Surely, that would take me out of the running for a job with God. I assumed my resume would go directly into a Heavenly shredder and Father would shout, "Next"!

What was so divine about me?

On my way home, I cried so hard I could barely see the road. Father kept speaking to me, trying to comfort me and I refused to acknowledge him. I would not give into my mental illness and listen to or answer the voices in my head.

With pure love and understanding, Father said "All is well, my sweet daughter. You and Ian will see the path to your happiness shortly." I only cried harder.

That same church leader would tell Ian and I one week later at our little meeting, that he had prayed about the story I shared with him. He said that God had told him that everything I had said was true and he was to help us in anyway possible. It was incredible to see how Father works.

Then, two months later, Ian and I would get summoned back into this man's office and told the "higher ups" in this church had instructed him to tell me once again that I could not hear God unless it was regarding my children. I was to cease and desist any spiritual healing or claims to hear God. The consequences of my actions would be death! I'm just kidding, they would kick me out of their church. Ian and I told him if we had to choose between God and an organization about God, we would choose God every time. It is hard to watch fear and judgement destroy truth and love.

I asked this holy man of God what had changed? Didn't God tell him personally that everything I had told him was true?

But he would not even meet my eyes as he placed his hands on his desk with a smile and said, "Well, I think this was all just a big misunderstand."

Just like my mother, he had dismissed us. Conversation over.

To be fair, this church leader is a good man. I still think of him often and love his Divine Spirt with intensity. But we could not allow our love for him to influence what God had asked us to do. So, Ian and I promptly chose God over man's ignorance and fear by removing our names from the membership rolls of that church.

We better get back to Ian and see if he knows who he wants to be yet!

Two weeks after Ian quit his job, I realized that our green wing Macaw, Maui, was out of chew toys. He was biting at his feathers and destroying them. I had to make a choice to spend sixty dollars on Maui's toy and save his feathers or keep the water on.

When I brought this dilemma to Ian's attention, he told me not to worry about it. He assured me he had some scrap wood in the garage and could make something Maui could entertain himself with so he would leave his feathers alone.

Ian spent the next three days in the garage making not just toys for Maui, but a wooden perch for our living room too.

He also made a shower perch for Maui so I would not have to continue to take him into the shower with me. It had become a nightmare trying to hold Maui under the water in the shower while he tries to splash around.

Then he made Maui a car seat. No, really, a car seat, for our bird. It was seriously cool.

After the third day making cool bird stuff in our garage, Ian walked inside and proclaimed, "I know who I want to be." I was so relieved I almost cried.

Finally, we could start receiving a paycheck again and I would not have to scrounge pennies to pay for gas so I could drive Jenae to school.

"Just tell me what you want to be my love! I already have your resume ready to go." I excitedly said to my husband.

"I want to go into business for myself and make things for large birds like Maui!" Ian said with complete confidence.

I stood there, smiling, and waiting for the punchline. He had to be kidding, right?

"I will only need a few thousand dollars to buy tools and supplies to get started." Ian continued excitedly.

"That sounds like a wonderful hobby honey and definitely something to work towards. But what do you want to do right now to earn a paycheck? You know, so we can eat and have electricity?" I said in a huff.

I start mentally preparing myself for the phone call I will have to make to my siblings.

Neither of them had contributed physically or financially with our mother's care in the last two years, not even a lunch date to give me a break. It was time for them to step up.

I had realized that I would need to get a job, today.

Ian had inhaled too much man glitter in the last three days, and now he is insane. I've heard sawdust can do that to a man.

I made a silent promise to Ian that I will do everything in my power to find a cure for man glitter exposure, no matter how long it takes.

"Are you listening to me?" Ian said interrupting the backup plan I had been forming in my head. "I want to build things to make a paycheck and I have always wanted to work for myself." I can see that he is getting annoyed at my lack of excitement.

I give Ian my 'I need a minute, or I will hurt your feelings' face and run up the staircase and into our room.

I am so furious that Ian has squandered the last two weeks while I have been scraping by to keep our household running on pennies and credit cards. The same credit cards we had just paid off.

Once in our room, I kneel at the foot of our bed and began to pray. Ok, to be honest, it was more like I began to vent.

"Father! Will you look at this mess? You and I gave Ian two weeks to decide who he wanted to be and look at what he has done!" I said, getting more and more livid by the second.

"There is no way we can spend thousands of dollars on tools. How will we pay bills while he is trying to build up customers? How could he be so selfish?" I continued, completely incensed.

Out of thin air I hear that male voice again. This time it is in a tone that I never want to hear again.

"MY CHILD, DID I ASK YOU ABOUT MONEY?" The voice said.

I very aware it is truly God speaking to me and he is not pleased.

"No Father, you did not." I quietly reply.

"DOES IAN KNOW WHO HE WANTS TO BE?" God questions sternly.

"Yes Father, he does." I say in barely a whisper.

"DID YOU SUPPORT HIM ON HIS DECISION?" Father asks in that same firm voice.

"No Father, I did not." I said, my voice almost inaudible from shame.

"Would you like a moment to do so my child?" Father said sounding a little less annoyed.

"Yes Father." I reply as I hastily get up to run down the stairs to apologize to Ian.

When I get out to the garage, Ian is already working on his next project. He was turning and old armoire into a birdcage. As I am watching him work, I realized that Ian is talented.

Finally, Ian notices that I have entered the garage and turns off the tool he is using and sets it down. I started to cry from the shame I felt and quickly move to embrace my husband. The same husband who has always supported my choices and differences, no matter what.

My soul mate who did not bat an eye when I told him that God had spoken to me. I knew I had been a complete jerk.

"I am so sorry Ian. I believe in you and I believe in us. There is nothing we can't do if we do it together. We will make this work." I humbly said.

Ian began to tell me of his plans for new products that he had coming into his head over the last three days. Ian had his joy back and I had almost ruined it with fear.

I went back upstairs to my room. I thanked Father for helping me to see what was important and apologized for my behavior.

Forty-eight hours later, Ian received a call from a family friend. This family friend told Ian that he heard Ian wanted to start his own business. This family friend asked Ian if that was true and what kind of business, he was thinking of starting.

Ian told his friend all about his exciting ideas and plans to work for himself. The sparkle was back in Ian's eyes while he discussed with his friend the tools and materials he would need to buy when we could get the money together.

"Ian, I would like to invest $10,000.00 interest free for a year in your new business." I heard Ian's friend say over the cellphone's speaker. "Would you like to come pick up the check now?"

I stood there, stunned and unable to process what had just happened, when I heard Father loving say, "You see my child, fear is not of me. I have already told you I will bring all that you need to your doorstep."

With tears of relief, joy and amazement running down my checks, all I can do is fall to my knees and whisper, "Thank you, Father, thank you".

CHAPTER FOUR

Even after the $10,000 check event, I was still struggling with whether I had a brain tumor. Or maybe I experienced a mild stroke or even possibly mental illness. I am getting older. It could have all just been a coincidence. Isn't that what society would say?

WebMD had given me a whole list of ailments, but my doctor had verified that none of them were the culprit of my improved hearing. That's what my doctor called it, improved hearing.

My doctor is a cool cat and believes me 100%. He made me prove it about two hundred times first, but we are past that now. I don't hold it against him; he is a man of science and just needed to see it with his own eyes. I agreed to his research, but only if there would be no needles.

Anyway, my doctor told me that if he wrote up my improved hearing as suddenly hearing God, the medical community would require him to give me a referral for a psych consultation. Apparently, it is in the doctor rule book.

No wonder humans live in constant fear of judgement. I think it is a travesty that our society teaches medical professionals that if a patient claims to hear God; they require mental health treatment!

A large part of my job is to teach people that we can all hear God like I do; We just need to understand how to listen. We all have the same ears! I hope the medical community has a sizeable supply of the little white jackets that tie in back because the Divine Spirit knows truth when it hears it.

But isn't that what I would say if I was mentally ill? That God spoke to me? Hasn't every religious cult started with some dude saying he could hear God and that God wants them all to drink the cool-aid?

God sent me another event on June 5, 2018 to make it perfectly clear I was hearing Father more and more clearly every day. This day would be key to helping me see firsthand the importance of forgiveness.

June 5, 2018 at 7:00 a.m., I sat bolt upright in my bed. I had startled Ian, and he sat up next to me in our bed.

"Are you okay?" Ian asked me with true concern in his voice, looking around for an intruder.

"I need to go to the grocery store and get some milk." I reply in a rush, while getting out of bed.

"We have milk babe." Ian said laying back down realizing that there is not an intruder in the house, his wife was just weird.

"I need to go to the grocery store over the bridge and get some milk." I stated again more sternly while I am quickly trying to find shoes.

Ian sat up cautiously and got out of bed. It is clear he seems concerned about my franticness as he carefully approaches me. He stood in front of me and tilted my head up so he could make eye contact with me.

"Honey, we have milk. I bought a whole gallon yesterday." Ian says in a very soothing tone. "Are you okay?" Ian asks me with apprehension.

"I HAVE TO GO TO THE GROCERY STORE RIGHT NOW AND GET MILK!!!" I scream as I am running out of the bedroom.

Ian stood stunned and confused as he watched me flee down the stairs towards the front door. He finally realizes my appearance as he tries to catch me before I run out the door.

"Are you going to brush your hair or teeth?" Ian shouts after me. "At least put a bra on!"

But I was already out the front door and running to the car. I had this feeling that if I did not go immediately, the entire world would cease to exist, and it would be my fault.

I drove directly to the grocery store as quickly as traffic would allow. When I got out of the car in the grocery store parking lot, my first thought was how grateful I was that I put flip flops on. It was June in south Texas and the pavement was steaming.

The urgency to get inside and to the milk aisle was so overwhelming that I began to run in the store's direction. That would be when I realized I did not have a bra on, and my flimsy summer jammies did not lend any support. I am not a small woman. Quite a few men and several women stopped to watch the show.

Two black eyes and several jobs offers later; I was running through the store towards the milk aisle. I came to a sudden stop in front of the milk and sensed I was in the wrong place. That was when my body just took on a life of its own. I turned around and began towards the butter aisle. I stopped right in front of this sweet little old man, innocently picking out his favorite butter.

I must describe the scene for you, so you can have a nice visual and a delightful laugh.

I wore my flimsy jammies and flip flops. I had not bothered taking the time to put on undergarments and I was standing in front of an open refrigerated cooler of butter. Anyone close realized that I was cold. I had not brushed my teeth or my hair.

Most days when I get up my hair looks like a troll head pencil topper. You know, the pencil topper that you smooth the hair down and then rapidly roll the pencil between your hands. Then when you complete rolling the pencil, the troll's hair looks like it didn't make it to the tornado shelter in time. Yeah, my hair looked like that. People of Walmart here I come! Do you have a good mental picture now?

I am always mentally aware and respectful of personal space, both mine and other peoples. My body did not seem to have the same awareness or respect today because my feet did not stop until I was almost touching this unsuspecting stranger. When I halted in front of him, he looked up from his butter and smiled at me, looking a bit confused by my nearness.

"May I touch your forehead?" I instantly say to this adorable little man as we make eye contact.

"Why yes, you may." the naïve elderly gentleman says to me, noticing my attire but not seeming to care.

No! You say, NO if an insane person asks to touch you! I think in my head. I am instantly concerned about this man's inability to detect crazy, even when it is standing right in front of him wearing jammies in the butter aisle. But I do not seem in control of my voice to recommend he take heed of this advice.

I reached out my right hand towards this brave soul standing before me. My thumb instinctually went right between his eyebrows where your third eye is.

I was not in control of where I placed my thumb or where this elusive third eye should supposedly be located. I had heard stories about this third eye phenomenon, but I thought it was more of a metaphorical thing.

This whole event felt like what I would imagine an out of body experience would feel like. The difference being that I was watching the events through my own eyes instead of floating above the room.

"Your Uncle Jerry sexually assaulted you when you were four years old. Is it okay if we heal that?" I hear myself say, matter of fact. It is the strangest feeling to have words come out of your mouth that you did not think or form in your head.

"Okay, but I believe Jerry is still alive." the trusting senior chap says as he nods his permission for me to continue the insanity. I'm guessing he thought I would channel a dead spirit or something along those lines.

I am already freaked out enough dude, did you need to put that thought in my head I remember thinking but said instead, in a small voice, "Okay." sounding almost apologetic. Again, some invisible force seemed to take over my actions and my words.

I looked into his amused and curious eyes. With my thumb on his forehead between his eyebrows I have the most overwhelming feeling of guilt and shame come over me. I knew it had not been my actions that took away this man's innocence, but it hurt my heart as if I had. I felt the guilt and shame like it was my own. It was so overwhelming that I felt like I couldn't breathe.

"I am so sorry for what I did to you as a child. I was so messed up on drugs and booze back then." I heard myself say in a tone and speech pattern that was not mine.

"There is no excuse for what I did to you, and I am so sorry. I have picked up the phone to call you a thousand times over the years to beg for your forgiveness." I continue with a feeling of urgency to get it all out before this man in front of me runs screaming for help.

"I want you to know that I checked into rehab the day after I hurt you and got clean. I have spent every day since then trying to save every child from the pain and suffering I so selfishly caused you."

It was right around this time that my stomach started to feel like I had butterflies fluttering around, but I continued to speak to this loving elderly man as we both began to weep.

"Can you please forgive me?" I ask as the butterflies seem to stop flutter and form a ball in my stomach, next to my belly button.

"Yes, I forgive you Jerry." the beautiful sweet soul before me utters softly through his tears.

As soon as he said the word yes, I felt a strong sensation that made me jump. It felt like someone had installed a zipper in my belly button and zipped up the center of my chest. The feeling was like the first plunge down on a roller coaster. It wasn't painful, but it was very shocking.

When I had startled from the sensation, I inadvertently took a step back, removing my thumb from my beloved new friend's forehead. The moment my thumb disconnected from his forehead, I was in complete control of my actions and voice, for the first time that day.

The man before me was staring at me with awe and amazement. He had tears silently streaming down his sweet wrinkled face. I was crying too.

It was a very sweet moment between us, but it distracted me when I notice we have attracted a crowd.

"Thank you. Thank you. What did you do? It doesn't hurt any more, what did you do? I have been trying for 60 years to take away the pain. What did you do?" the humble man keeps repeating while searching my face for answers."

I was just about to say I don't know when suddenly, I knew what had happened. I knew exactly what it was.

"I healed a fracture in your Divine Spirt." I said just as amazed as the man before me. We both stood there in stunned silence for a moment.

"How?" He finally asks me, pleading for answers. Once again, I opened my mouth to say I don't know but I knew how. I knew it with a surety that could not be shook.

I looked directly into his eyes and stated proudly, "God".

This sweet angel in human form, smiled at me with the most intense love and gratitude, then hugged me so tight it broke the spell I had been in.

I immediately know that the small crowd I had noticed a moment ago, had grown into a large crowd. Looking around at the curious faces, I suddenly remember the state of my appearance. It mortified me. I quickly turned away from the man and crowd and ran, sobbing to my car.

"I saw the angel in your eyes." The sweet little old man shouted after me. I guess he felt sorry for me because of my appearance and wanted to compliment my blue eyes.

After reaching my car, I got in and turned the air conditioner on full blast. I sat there in my car for what seemed like hours crying and shaking. There was now absolutely no doubt in my mind. I am insane.

I went to reach for my phone to call Ian. My hero would come and get me. He could take me to the emergency room and explain to the doctor about by decline into madness.

It was then that I realized that I had left the house without my phone or purse. As I take a deep breath, I tell myself to calm down. I could drive myself home.

I was so bewildered at what had just transpired in the butter aisle of the grocery store and I just wanted to get home to Ian. Slowly, I put my car in drive and began the fifteen-minute trip home, forcing myself not to focus on anything other than the route home.

When I pulled into the driveway, I was so physically exhausted that I had to sit in the car for another twenty minutes to get the energy to walk from the car to the front door.

Finally, I forced myself to get out of the car. As I am trying to focus on the front door, I know that I am walking unsteady as if I was drunk. I could not understand why I felt so physically weak. When I finally got to the door, I could see it was magically opening on its own.

There stood my hero, my warrior, Ian. Everything would be okay now. We would figure this out together when I wasn't so tired, and I could think straight. He would know what to say!

"Where's the milk?" Ian asked confused at my unsteady gait. Really Ian? Where's the milk? I thought.

I know that I am safe now and collapse just inside the door. As Ian reaches out to catch me, he is looking around with panic in his face. He already had worry about my behavior before I left and now, I was a complete train wreck.

I instantly begin to cry as Ian is scanning my entire body, looking for any injuries to explain the disaster I have dissolved into.

Ian knows it must be bad for me to be so completely out of it. I am normally the one who handles every catastrophe because I just instinctually know how to fix everything.

I lay there in the foyer while recounting to Ian everything that had happened from the moment, I woke up this morning. I explained that I was so tired I was having a hard time focusing on speaking to him. I had assumed it was from crying so much over the last hour.

Ian helped me up to our bedroom so I could lie down. I was so tired I could not keep my eyes open a moment longer and I was asleep when my head hit my pillow.

Amazingly, I slept for seven days. Not seven hours, seven days.

My poor sweet Ian was so worried. He would habitually wake me up four or five times a day to make sure I was eating and drinking, then help me to the bathroom. Just that minimal effort would make me so tired again that I would instantly fall back asleep.

Ian continued to ask me if he should take me to the emergency room or my doctor. Somehow, I knew I was okay and that I just needed to sleep. It was hard stay awake long enough to explain this to Ian. Then, seven days later, I was good. I woke up on the morning of the seventh day and felt refreshed.

The instant my eyes opened; I knew exactly what had happened at the grocery store. I had complete knowledge of what a fracture in our Divine Spirit was and how to heal it. I knew why it was necessary to heal the fractures. I realized how vital forgiveness was to our eternal peace, love and joy.

As I explained all of this to Ian, my mind was racing. We could change the entire world with this knowledge. We could end the need for wars and cruelty.

It took almost three weeks this time to convince myself that I was crazy and needed another CT scan of my brain to check for a tumor.

What was so divine about me I thought God was talking to me and that I could change the world? How could forgiveness be the key to peace, love and joy? I am just one person, what could I possibly do?

Father was about to show me, with Him, we can all do the impossible.

CHAPTER FIVE

July 5, 2018

The morning began normally enough for my husband, Ian, and me. We were discussing our plans for the day while lying in bed facing one another.

We had learned early on when our two beautiful girls were little, that this time alone would be the only time in the day we would have each other's full attention with no distractions. This also allowed us to synchronize our watches for the day's events.

Although both girls were now adults, it had become a habit over the last 23 years. It was my favorite part of my day; Ian is beautiful to look at.

"So…do you feel the need to leap up and dash to the grocery store to acquire any dairy products? But then not buy anything to bring home?" my husband jokingly asked.

I give him my best "you're so funny" look as I notice his eyes widen to the size of saucers. Ian is focusing on something just over my left shoulder.

Thinking we are still in "being funny" mode, I ask in an exaggerated and quivering voice if he is staring at a monster behind me? He says nothing and continues to stare.

I felt a little uneasy as my husband is a 20-year Army veteran and does not show fear often, if ever. I cautiously ask him, "No really, is there a monster behind me?". He said nothing, continuing to just stare without blinking.

Trying to tap down the panic I am feeling, I jokingly make a comment like, "Some warrior you are, I guess I will have to kill the monster myself!" Then I turned to see what had him so mesmerized.

It took a minute for my brain to register that right in front of me, about four feet off the ground next to my bed, was a large ball of white light.

It is the size of a large beach ball and is the most brilliant white I have ever seen. It was so radiant that it was a complete absence of darkness to the point of iridescence, while having the characteristics of a rainbow.

I remember feeling no fear, just fascination and thinking it was so bright that I should get my sunglasses while I examine this odd sight floating next to my bed. The only other thought I remember having at that moment was, you don't see that every day.

No sooner did that thought enter my mind, the shape began to elongate, and turn into a more human like silhouette, but still that brilliant white color.

Finally, after what seemed like hours, the white ball had taken a human shape but with no specific features. This human looking form then sat on my bed next to me. I feel the weight of a person sitting down in front of me on my bed, as my husband and children have done thousands of times over the years.

I looked up in fascination into the mostly featureless face of this being and observed the most enchanting blue eyes ever created. I know they were blue, but not any shade of blue that I have seen in my human existence, they were so beautiful and vibrant. I know I have seen this blue before, just not on earth.

I began to cry tears of love and joy because I instantly knew the Being before me.

I smiled through my tears and said, "Hello Father."

I don't mean my dearly departed earthly father, I was looking into the eyes of my Heavenly Father, the God of all creation, God, The Father.

I did not see but felt Father smile as he replied to me, "Hello my daughter. It is time." I instantly looked at the clock which read 9 a.m.

"Time for what Father?" I asked a little bit confused.

At that moment, it occurred to me that I was still lying down under my covers. I sat up suddenly and looked down at my husband, realized he was still lying next to me, and still staring at this amazing site before us.

I leaned down and whispered to him, "You see this right"?

Those words seemed to pull him out of the trance he had been in and as he sat up next to me, he whispered back, "Uh-huh".

I am a little embarrassed to say that we continued to whisper between us. Both of us trying to be sure the other one was seeing this incredible sight.

I would love to report that we stopped acting like star struck teenagers over the next 3 hours, but that would not be the truth.

To this day the memory of us whispering back and forth to each other, in front of God, as if he could not hear us, will always bring a smile and a lot of laughter on the rough days.

How naïve we were on "God Protocol" then.

I like to joke that God must have, in that three hours, put his hands over his face while repeatedly murmuring to himself, "Patience is one of my virtues." But in true God fashion he has blocked that memory from our human minds. God is cool like that.

He is always doing things to help us to feel peace, love and joy and to remove fear.

CHAPTER SIX

So, what did God talk to us about for the next three hours you may wonder?

He talked to us about the TRUTH, His truth. He described to us in astonishing detail what was coming and what we would need to do.

Father explained to us that ALL His children are born divine and of worth, and that it is society that shouts to us we are not enough. Out of fear of judgement and fear of failure, we listen.

We strive to become what society tells us people will respect instead of becoming the person we would respect.

Father's eyes then seemed to fill with hurt and sadness as he shared with us that over time, so much Heavenly truth continued to be hidden, lost and even stolen.

He told us of the multitude of truth removed from the bible and other writings because of pride, greed and ignorance. He explained that man has also eradicated anything that seemed fanciful or magical over the years.

Those in power would excuse truth being removed from history by stating it was for everyone's own good. It seemed they believed that humans are just too fragile and weak minded to handle the full truth.

"The truth of their actions was not so noble as this." Father said.

"When man became so very cruel and worldly, the richest of whom were the rulers, they began to covet and hide my truth to enslave my children. Many who claimed to know my word would demand gold and goods for the 'privilege' to hear the truth. Most of the time however, it was more fear to control my children, keeping the truth hidden away. They believed nobility to be the only humans to be worthy of my truth while disregarding the elements of truth that did not please them." Father continued.

He told us that many of his children came directly to Him for answers and lived lives of peace, love and joy. But many others did not and fell prey to the lies that lead to a lifetime of fear on earth. Father said that they removed even the writings about our Heavenly Mother, His wife.

"Wait, what? You have a wife?" I gasped.

Father smiled at me because he knew I was already aware, for many years now, that Heavenly Mother was sitting next to Him in heaven. I made the joke because it seems to be a very controversial subject. He said to us he does not understand why it is so hard for humans to believe that He has a wife.

"Did I not explain that all would be done on earth as it is in heaven?" Father asked. He continued by saying, "Why would you be sent to earth with the instinct to have a mate and reproduce if it were not the same in heaven? If I created all your spirits alone, would you not be able to create your children alone, without a mate?"

He expressed his disappointment with the fact that all crucial historical information about women would be removed because of fear and hatred, something that I will go into more detail in my next book.

He described how skewed and perverted his words and character have become, telling us sadly that the darkness loves to shout what a JEALOUS AND VENGEFUL God He is.

This act is to spread fear and deter each of us from the desire to hear our Father in Heaven and so many of us believe it. But He is just a dad, that loves us, and wants more than anything for us to be happy.

There are only a few things we can do on earth that will get Father riled up. When I asked Him which one displeases Him the most, He became quiet for a long moment.

I was just about to apologize if I had overstepped with my question when he answered.

"The most tragic transgression is for one to convince another that I do not exist. It is not because of arrogance that I say this but for the sadness of the soul that stops growing. It is a great hindrance to the soul that ceases expanding during life on earth, for they must continue that growth before the next period of glory can begin for them." Father explained.

"The growth on earth that is possible to obtain in eighty years will take the equivalent of eighty million years in the next realm. Time does not exist in the heavenly realm, so it is impossible for me to explain this further." Father said.

I asked God, "So if I tell someone you are not real, and they believe me, I should expect a smack down in heaven?" I joked.

"I am fully mindful that you have never doubted me, but only yourself, my child." Father chuckled. "But there are other methods used to blot me from the minds of my children." He said with what seemed to be a mixture of sadness and annoyance.

Ian and I both looked to the other for clarification. Father could see that we did not understand another way to accomplish this, so he expounded.

"I gave one absolute promise to each of my children. The promise that I would NEVER take your freewill to choose your path on earth, it is ingrained in your Divine Spirit. It is the reason that anytime you feel that you are being pressed to go against your desired path, you will resist. Now imagine the effect on the human mind if you are continuously surrounded in judgement and fear as you attempt to follow your desired path. All the while being told that it is my will and word that you are being judged by. By nature, you would be forced to change your desired path or come to believe I must not exist so you may find your peace, love and joy." Father stated.

Trying to be sure I understood His meaning I clarified by asking, "So, raising a child in an environment and told that you, God, will not love them if they do not follow certain guidelines, that Divine Spirit is having freewill taken and the blame put on God for a human's actions?"

"There will always be those who attempt to create fear to scare my children into relinquishing their freewill by threats of hell or damnation. But are they not attempting to undo the promise I have made? The promise to all my children to never take freewill. Are they not attempting to put their will above The God of Creation? If they indeed had my truth, they would know that fear is not of me and they would not spread it. If they indeed had my truth, they would know that the authority to judge does not reside on the earth and they would not do it." Father stated sternly.

He continued by saying "Therefore, the act of spreading fear, hate or judgement disguised as my word to coerce any of my children into surrendering their freewill, will be seen by the Heavens as an attempt to put one's self before Me, the God of Creation and therefore breaking the first commandment."

No one breaks it down Barney style like God! Ian and I both sat in stunned silence as we took in Father's words and his meaning.

The first commandment says, "Thou shall put no other Gods before me." I started to think about how I have judged others and been unkind in my life, at times. I could feel the disappointment Father felt that any of His beloved children would indulge in judgement and spreading fear. I made a mental note that I would need to be sure that I never repeated that behavior again.

"It is the responsibility of each Divine Spirit to speak their truth with no fear of judgement. It is not your place to convince another of the validity of your truth as this would be akin to attempting to take freewill. When you speak your truth to another, their Divine Spirit will know it to be truth or they can reject it if they choose. The truth NEVER has to be defended my child, because it just is." Father passionately shared with Ian and me.

He continued with this line of thought by helping us to understand that we are not less if someone does not agree with us. That we are all allowed our own truth. But just as we have the right to our truth with no judgement, so does everyone else. If we desire to speak our truth and not judged, then we must allow the same for others, even if we disagree.

That does not mean you have to concede on a matter that you do not agree with. What it means is that you should speak your truth in a polite and respectful manner without fear and allow others to do the same, without judgement. To be respectful of each other's views, which will turn a confrontation into a conversation.

When we listen to an opposing view without the need to form a rebuttal, we can truly hear what is being said. Isn't that what you would like others to do for you? To listen to you when you speak instead of just crafting a response?

If I like vanilla ice cream and you like chocolate ice cream, which one of us is wrong? If I cannot convince you to prefer vanilla, am I less? We are all allowed to have our own truth, with no judgement!

Father gave Ian and I a simple guideline to help us always check our actions and be sure we are not being judgmental. He told us that if you add a label or an action to the person or event, it is judgement. Let me explain that with an example.

If I were to say that I believe that pedophilia is wrong, that is my opinion. Which, because of freewill, I am allowed my own opinion. If I were to say that all pedophiles are dirtbags, that would put a label on it and judgement. If I were to say that all pedophiles should get the death penalty, that would put an action to it and judgement.

"How did I not know all of this Father? Why is this not common knowledge to every human being?" I asked, completely exasperated.

He explained how as humans we have become reliant on man or "society" to tell us what God's will is, instead of asking Him ourselves. Sometimes, that lack of communication with Father is out of self-doubt that we surely cannot hear Him ourselves, and other times the false fear that there will be consequences for us if we are wrong.

Father shared with us He does not dispense punishment on the earth. He also said that each one of us can hear Him as if He were standing next to us.

He told us that society has taught so many of his children, from birth, that you must be a certain gender, a certain age, a certain faith, single, married, gay, straight, licensed, schooled, layman, set apart, set upon or just plain born into divinity to hear Father personally.

He said there have been more lies told to convince humans we are not worthy enough to hear our own Father in Heaven, than there has been truth spoken to teach each of us how to hear him perfectly clear.

Father would tell us that the greatest challenge each of His children struggle to overcome is fear. He told us that fear is not of Him and that fear is a lie 100% of the time. I jokingly said to Father that I believed that a little fear is good to keep us motivated.

"As a mother, do you want your children to feel fear or to be aware and respectful?" Father questioned me clearly.

"Aware and respectful of course." I replied.

"Am I a lesser parent than you my child?" Father softly asked.

"No Father, you are not." I humbly reply.

He then softly said, "But yet you have so easily believed what society has told you about how to interpret my word instead of asking me directly, have you not? Was that aware and respectful or out of fear?"

I was too ashamed to answer this last question because he was right, I had allowed society to tell me what the words in the bible and other scriptures meant without once asking Father for clarification.

"Fear is not of me my child; fear is not truth" Father said emphatically. "If fear is not truth, why would you plan your path on earth by fear?"

"Look back at your life my child, was not every choice you regret rooted in fear? Fear of judgement, fear of consequences, fear of failure, fear of loss?" He went on say that fear is the ONLY way that negative energy can attach to you.

You cannot invite it in, they cannot put it upon you, you cannot walk through a 'haunted' building and have it jump on you. Fear is the only way to let negative energy into your Divine Spirit. When we allow fear, it creates an opening into your Divine Spirit which will give the dark energy an access point.

He also said that the phrase 'do not fear' is in the bible 365 times, once for every day of the year. I believe it was Father's way to help us know how important not allowing fear would be for our lives here on earth.

I did not count how many 'do not fear' were in the bible myself, but I googled it. Google confirmed that the phrase 'do not fear' is in the bible 365 times, not that I thought God had it wrong.

Father continued to explain the negative side effects of fear by saying, "Fear allows anger and anger hides fear, neither of which are truth."

He could see the confused look on Ian and my face as we tried to understand what was being said.

Father clarified by saying, "Anger is the easiest emotion to experience and the only emotion that has no loss attached to it. If the anger leaves, you feel better, if the anger gets worse, you feel more justified."

"All other emotions have the potential to produce emotional pain." Father continued. "If you love something, it can be lost. If you are full of joy, it can be taken. If you are sad, it can be made worse."

"Fear is the hardest emotion to feel because it is not of me and therefore not truth. It is unnatural and foreign to the Divine Spirit and therefore the most uncomfortable to feel." Father explained.

Father continued by saying, "So, it is human nature to process fear through the most comfortable filter, which is anger."

Let me give you an example to hopefully clarify the point Father was making.

A few years ago, I was quite overweight. If Ian would have said to me, "Do you really think you need another donut?" as I was reaching for my fourth one, I would have been livid because of my fear of how people perceived my physical appearance.

If Ian were to say the same thing today, I would laugh and tell him I needed the whole box. What has changed? I have lost some weight, but I'm still a big girl. The difference is that I no longer FEAR how people perceive my physical body. No fear, no anger. That works for me!

Father taught Ian and me that when you get angry, find the fear you are hiding from so you can remove it for good. Remembering that fear is a lie 100% of the time. As you remove fear from your life, peace, love and joy will start forming right before your eyes.

Imagine never feeling that pit of fear in your stomach for the rest of your life on earth!

Ian and I have watched this miracle emerge in our own lives over the last year.

Father said, "Just as you cannot have complete light if there is darkness, you cannot have complete darkness if there is light. Peace, love and joy is the ABSENCE of fear. All will be balanced without fear." Father revealed.

Father needed for Ian and me to know how to remove fear because of what he would share with us next.

When Father began explaining to Ian and me what this path would require us to accomplish, I was trying to fight off the fear of failure on a scale I never believed I would ever experience. It was all overwhelming to my human brain.

God, Himself was sitting on my bed speaking to my husband and me. I could not convince myself this time that it was a brain tumor or mental illness. I could no longer hide from what I was being called to do.

I tried to focus on Father's voice, as He cautioned us about the constant and intense judgement we would face and the potential fear that judgement may evoke within us.

He told us the cruelty and ridicule we would endure would be on a level that would rival my childhood. It would come from every area of our human lives from our family, friends, and even strangers. But most of all, fellow church members who may not respect our freewill as we change our belief system.

Father told us that there will be many that claim to love and follow Him and His beloved Son Christ, while using Father and Christ as their authority to pass judgement and spread hate to stop truth.

Father was very clear that this would be part of what we would face, if we chose the path, he was laying out in front of us. This part did not sound pleasant at all. Father reminded us that man had been using fear to control God's children since the beginning of time.

I began to have a troubling thought trying to make its way into my brain. I was remembering the recent events taking place over the past few years throughout the world. There had been so many incidents involving acts of bloodshed against human beings by human beings.

The general attitude of the world seems to have come to the belief that if something or someone is different or offends you, you must cancel it or discredit it. If you cannot cancel it or discredit it, then you somehow have the right to kill it.

This was a mark in the 'not today' column. I was very naïve back then and imagined that Ian and I would only have truth and our love as a shield for our fragile human brains and even more fragile bodies.

This was not a reassuring thought. But we would have each other and we would have Father. That is more than most people know that they have.

Father was clear on how truly hard and emotionally painful some of the events would be. He also wanted us to know how amazing a lot of it would be.

It was VITAL for us to understand the level of resistance the darkness would provide for our journey to bring the world

Father's truth. But also, that we had agreed to this path before our Divine Spirits and human bodies came together on this earth.

We had agreed to assist Father to bring His children home to him, with truth.

"Why me, Father? I get how Ian is divine, that's why I chose him as my husband. But why me? What have I ever done to make you believe that I am worthy of your love and trust? What is so divine about me Father?"

Father smiled at me and said, "What is so divine about you my child? Nothing and everything. You are no better than any other, you are just different. Why have I come to you this day, my precious daughter? Because you said you would."

CHAPTER SEVEN

It was then that Father showed Ian and I what he meant by the phrase, because you said you would. He showed us how He and Heavenly Mother stood face to face with their hands held out in front of them palms up and fingertips touching.

We watched as a dazzling ball of white light with little gold flecks in it began to form just above their upturned palms as they starred into each other's eyes with pure love.

The gold flecks looked like a sparkler that you would give a young child on the fourth of July. When the white ball of light was about as big as a beach ball, they placed it at their feet and began the entire process all over again.

Father told us they create every Divine Spirit this way. He then allowed us to re-live events in heaven that all of us were a part of before He placed our Divine Spirits in human bodies to come to earth.

He showed Ian and I that every Divine Spirit had chosen a path and lessons that each individual spirit wanted to learn hoping to become more like our Father and Mother in Heaven.

He explained how He created everything, including our Divine Spirit and our physical body. Then each of us chose what we wanted to learn and experience while here on earth.

Father broke it down to the simplest form by saying, "Imagine it this way, I, God, created the Monopoly board, the cards, the fake money and the pieces you move around the board to represent your progress in the game. You chose which piece to represent you during your human life and how you desired to play. Some Divine Spirits had only one goal, to avoid landing on the 'Go Directly to Jail' space. Some wanted to focus on regularly passing the "Go" in order to collect their $200 and nothing else. Some wanted to own "Boardwalk and Park Place" with all hotels in the hopes of controlling the entire board, while others wanted to be the banker, and still others wanted to bet everything in hopes of landing on free parking."

He continued on to say, "I, God, did not intervene with the plans every Divine Spirit made for themselves, but remained available to each of you for guidance should any of my children ask. Remember that I made one absolute promise to each of you. I promised that I would NEVER take your FREEWILL. That you would be allowed to plan and execute your path and lessons as you choose. I gave some very simple rules that must be followed that each Divine Spirit agreed to. Most importantly, each Divine Spirit chose a trigger point for themselves. What that means is that I would not change anyone's plan unless the individual Divine Spirit asked me by name to intervene. My 'job' if you will, would be to put signs on earth to help remind each individual Divine Spirit what lessons THEY chose. This would enable them to create THEIR OWN peace, love and joy."

Father had to remind Ian and I that day of every truth that would affect our path so it could prepare us for the question that would forever change our lives and how we would see this world. It would shift my own personal understanding and perception of every living being on earth.

When Father had finished all he had to say about the truth of events from the past, about our future direction, and what we must do to complete Father's task that we had already agreed to in heaven, he was silent for a moment. I believe he was allowing me to gather myself and my thoughts.

When he could see that I was focusing on him again and eager to hear his next words, he trained those vibrant blue eyes upon me again and asked, "Do you accept this my child?"

As I said before, you may think this is a simple question that has a simple answer. It is God after all. It's not like I could tell him I was hoping to work on my tan that summer or suggest that maybe we revisit the issue after the holidays.

This is God, and he wants an answer. Right now.

I wasn't sure what the 'chatting with God sitting on the edge of your bed' etiquette was exactly. I didn't remember covering this in Sunday School, not even once. I may overstate my abilities when I was a child to pay attention and keep important information, but I really feel like this would be something I would have retained over the years.

So, I was not sure if He would consider it rude or disrespectful to ask for more time to think about it or if I could get some clarification on a few points?

Could I truly ask God if this would be part-time or full-time gig? Is this something I can do from home or will I need to travel? What percentage of the time would the travel be? Do you provide medical, dental and vision? Is this position considered management level or would this be more of an entry level thing? Any room for advancement? Do I have to die for advancement opportunities? Ian won't be boss right?

Wait, will I have to quit smoking? What about cussing or tattoos? Ian drinks beer, will that be a problem? We are only human after all.

But the intense peace, love and joy which is the absence of fear that he promised was a good selling point. All our fears were lies to keep us ignorant of Father's truth.

So, with a nod, I humbly said, "Yes Father. I accept."

I instantly felt the peace, love and joy that Father had promised would come over me. It came in a wave that was so intense I almost didn't hear His next words. It was as if every fear I had ever felt, just melted away.

All my life society has taught me I must have faith that Father is there and to hope he will bless me with his forgiveness and mercy. To hope I could someday be "worthy" of his love. I suddenly knew that there was something more than faith. This was not faith or hope, it was actual KNOWING. With knowing, you do not hope He is there; you know with a certainty He is there and will guide you to peace, love and joy.

You suddenly know that you were BORN worthy of his love and grace. That you need not seek his mercy for He does not punish us here on earth for using our freewill.

You know that He would never punish us for using the gift that HE gave to us, with the promise to never take it?

I felt a sense of knowing that I was unaware was even possible on earth. It was a knowing of Father with a surety that could not be shook. I explain the difference between faith and knowing to my clients with the following comparison.

Father appears to you and explains He wants you to drive 100 miles in your car, knowing your gas tank is on empty. He has a five-dollar bill in his hand to give to you for gas. The person with faith would gingerly take the money from Father, careful to make sure to immediately put it in a safe place. Faith would then cautiously get in their car and adjust their seat and mirror while looking down at the gas gauge. They would carefully exit their driveway and begin down the road, vigilant to not drive to use more gas than necessary.

The person with faith would make their first stop the gas station and put the entire five dollars in the gas tank, praying the entire time that it will be enough. Faith will then say another prayer while telling themselves they have faith that they will make it. Faith will check the gas gauge every few minutes the entire 100 miles.

The person with knowing would first, scream with excitement that Father is sending them on a new adventure. Then knowing would tell Father to keep the five-dollar bill while running to the car. Knowing would then squeal their tires while flying out of the driveway and then slam on gas, gunning the engine before speeding down the road.

The person with knowing would drive like their hair was on fire for 100 miles and never once look at the gas gauge, because they know with a surety that cannot be shook that Father will never ask them to go down a path that He hasn't already cleared the way for.

I felt as though I was about to explode with the Heavenly Energy coursing through me when Father focused those intense blue eyes on me again, and I knew that the words He was about to speak were VITAL for me to remember.

Father said in a very clear and firm voice, "My Child, from this day forward you will be known as my Oracle. You will not lie, you will not cheat, you will not steal, you will do NOTHING to disgrace my name."

Strangely enough, the words did not surprise me. It was almost as if I was expecting them even though I was not sure what an Oracle was. I've seen the Matrix like everybody else, but was that a true and accurate portrayal of an Oracle?

Instantly memories from my childhood began to flood back to me. These memories were not of fear or terror though.

They were memories of a man standing with me in the long line of evergreen and pine trees that my adoptive father had referred to as a shelter belt. This shelter belt was on that farm where so much sadness and horror had occurred when I was a child. Where the massacre of my beloved barbie Susan and her girls occurred.

I spent much of my time in that shelter belt while making friends with all the horses and cows that lived on our little farm. The animals were my loving family and the shelter belt was my safe space. I could escape from the terror that awaited me inside the house while spending time with my animal family.

The animals would always be happy to see me. They truly accepted me for me, not caring that I was different. They gave me the one thing I had craved most since the day my mother took my dad from me, unconditional love.

Each day when I would make my way to the tree line, my posse of cats would follow me. At first, I thought it was to sample my mud pies, they were exceptional. Then I decided that I must be a cat whisperer because they just followed me, no questions asked.

I would make the most amazing muds pies while talking to the cats, in those trees. I would also listen to the most amazing stories told by my very best friend.

In blocking out my childhood, I had also blocked out my very best friend! I began to cry with gratitude at the memory of my one true friend as a child.

My very best friend, that is was what I called him, showed up in the shelter belt one day. One minute I was alone then suddenly, he just appeared.

I had a close call that day with my brother during one of his assassination attempts. I zigged when I should have zagged and fallen while trying to get away. I told you zig zag running was an important skill!

I cut my leg bad and could not get it to stop bleeding. I could not go into the house to get first aid supplies or water to clean it for at least another hour. That would be when my adoptive father should get home. I hope I didn't leave a blood trail I thought to myself as I was putting pressure on my leg to slow down the bleeding.

No sooner did I have that thought when my very best friend just appeared in front of me with a bucket of water and bandages.

He never told me why he was there, and I never asked. I never even thought to ask why. It just seemed normal, like he had always been there. I always felt safe and peaceful when He was there, and I wasn't alone anymore.

He would tell me amazing stories about a rainstorm that caused a huge flood, a guy with a big magic stick that could make water part to save his friends from some bad guys, and a dude on his boat that got swallowed by a huge whale and then shot out the blow hole of the whale. I told my very best friend that I could relate to the whale and the blow hole because sometimes I have big poops too.

He was so patient when he explained to me what a blow hole was.

Sometimes my very best friend would stay the night in my room with me. It wasn't something arranged ahead of time. I never even thought to ask my mom for permission, she couldn't see him.

Actually, no one could see him but me. We would play for hours together and talk about everything that came to my immature mind.

He was always there and holding my hand when the monster came into my room at night. My very best friend would distract me by telling me stories about a brave woman and a mighty warrior that would someday speak God's truth and teach all of God's children to hear Him so they could live in peace, love and joy.

I would ask my very best friend if he thought brave woman and her warrior would come and help me live in peace, love and joy. He would always answer the same way.

"That brave woman has been with you since the day you were born child. Her warrior will appear when you are ready to see him." He would say.

I didn't understand what all of that meant but the words comforted me, so I didn't ask him to explain them.

On the unbearably bad nights with the monster in my room, my very best friend would distract me by showing me a magnificent garden with a golden river that he called the essence of life.

There was a beautiful woman with the most loving and kind smile that was always in that garden waiting for us to arrive. She would hold out her arms for an affectionate hug when she saw me.

After the monster would leave my room, my very best friend would hold me and cry with me. My very best friend was the same being that was standing in front of me now.

My very best friend was God.

He had been with me through all of it.

He had placed the piles of hay in just the right spot to catch me as my brother tossed me off the barn.

My very best friend had given me breath while I was being held under water.

He had calmed the horse every time my brother had spooked the horse.

He had made the gun misfire the day I fell and cut my leg, giving me time to get away.

He had held my hand during the worst moments in my life. Just as God and I had agreed upon before I ever came to this earth.

I remembered all of it.

It was as if Father had downloaded a massive new computer program in my brain that removed all the false data. It was a clarity and a knowing that I cannot describe in human words.

I fully knew of what my future path would be and that healing fractures in the Divine Spirits would be a large part of that. I would speak truth, Father's truth, which I now remembered was my truth too.

It would be my job to speak my truth with no fear of judgement. It would NOT be my job to force or convince anyone to believe it. Just to allow other Divine Spirits to hear it and to use their freewill to decide their path, with no judgement.

If it feels like truth to them, that is awesome. If it does not feel like their truth, that is okay too. There would be no need to decide who was right or who was wrong. We are all born more than enough to be exactly who we chose to be.

It is not my place to make you believe me, but to give you the information to decide for yourself. And to love the person you chose to be, even if I disagree.

I am human and flawed just like EVERYONE else. So, what is divine about me? Nothing and everything, the same as you. We are all the same and we are all different. No human is more vital than another. This process will be a lifetime of learning for me.

I am working towards and will someday be able to love the monster for being the adversity I needed in my life as a child. It was so vital for me to grow into the brave woman I heard stories about from my very best friend.

Society tells us from birth that everyone must be the same with identical desires and wants. This is a lie! Each Divine Spirit has a specific path that they chose for themselves before they ever came to this earth.

If everyone had only the desire to work at McDonald's, who would raise the cows to make the burgers? Who would God love more? The farmer or the worker making fries?

The answer is He loves both the farmer and the maker of fries the same. He loves me and you, the same.

He told Ian and I that often He sends people instead of events to provide the signs to point his children to their own peace, love and joy.

Father said to me, "I know you as a mother. I have watched as you have asked one of your beautiful children to speak to their sibling on your behalf when you could see that you were not speaking in a manner that your child could understand. I, your Father in Heaven, do this as well. My daughter, I must ask, would you then be silent when your child was ready to speak to you? Again, my child, am I a lesser parent than you?"

"No Father, you are not!" I proudly said.

Father is constantly speaking to all of us. He loves us exactly as we are and only wants our happiness. He is just a dad. A dad that loves His children.

CHAPTER EIGHT

I had so much information running through my brain and so many questions that I could not focus on just one. Father knew I was over loading; He has that whole perfect knowledge thing going on. He is cool like that.

To distract us and focus our brains, He began to explain to us about Oracles. He clarified that an Oracle is simply 'One who speaks GOD'S truth'.

He shared with Ian and me the truth about the treatment of Oracles throughout the years, and it was not a happy tale.

He described how Kings and Queens, Rulers of Nations and religious leaders would covet Oracles. They sequestered them by placing them in temples, castles, dungeons and even sometimes prisons.

He told us that once an Oracle's ability to hear Father appeared, those in power instantly began to manipulate the Oracle into a life of servitude to them instead of God. They did this to obtain gold and power while saying it was for the Oracles safety. But really, they were charging God's children to hear God's truth from the Oracle in order to line their own pockets with Gold.

Some Oracles did not fight the imprisonment, as Oracles are human and have the same right to freewill promised by God. But most of the Oracles requested God free them, often in the most volatile and corrupt locations on earth so they could spread the truth to His children and allow them to accept it or not with no judgement.

Father informed us that every time his children become so lost that the truth is in danger of disappearing completely, he will send Oracles to spread his truth again. He sends Oracles to give his children every opportunity to hear HIS TRUTH before any Heavenly event.

Father could see that we were trying to understand His words and picture what a Heavenly event would look like.

"Allow me to show you." Father said.

Right in front of our eyes, as if it was happening in our bedroom, we saw a disgusting, disturbing scene.

We saw men, women and children being beaten, raped and murdered by a massive group of people. It seemed as if they had all gone insane and lost their humanity.

It was not just men committing these horrendous acts, but men and women, from teenagers to the elderly. I was so shocked at the vision in front of me I grabbed onto my husband and tried to bury my face in his shoulder.

Father gently spoke to us saying, "I know it is difficult to experience, but you must both know the truth of the past so that you can be aware for what you may face in the future." Before I could ask the question burning in my heart Father spoke again.

"I am not condemning you to this future, only giving you the understanding of the importance of your task together. An awareness of the power of my truth. To have a complete understanding that you must never give up no matter the obstacle or fear. The true importance of NEVER allowing FEAR. To replace the fear with a knowing that I will guide you to where you need to be and open all necessary doors and boarders for as long as you request my assistance."

Reluctantly, I turned back to the movie playing out before me. I tried very hard not to focus on any specific person being tortured, but to take in the scene in its entirety.

I realized that I could physically feel the terror and pain of the innocent being brutalized if I focused on just one person. It was as if I was living the nightmare with them.

Once I could get my sorrow of the event under control, I found my focus being continuously drawn to one woman. I had never seen her before on earth, but I sensed that I knew her. It was her eyes, or rather the light in her eyes that kept drawing me to her.

They were not the Heavenly color of blue that I had seen in Father's eyes, but almost as beautiful. Her eyes continued to change from a dark blue to a pale blue. Watching her eyes transition between the two colors every few moments was both strange and amazing.

The twenty or more crazed people in the crowd around her repeatedly chanted, "REPENT, REPENT, REPENT!"

I finally realized the reason I was so drawn to her; she was the only person that seemed to have no fear. And her eyes. She was silent and had a sense of complete peace surrounding her.

While the mob continued to scream at her, they were kicking and hitting her as well. Some of the throng of madmen did not stop at just using fists and feet. They began stabbing this innocent woman with other sharp looking weapons.

She had no physical reaction and uttered no sounds. She did not cry out in pain, nor did she plead for them to stop. She did not resist in anyway.

She just sat on the ground, with her eyes staring at nothing as if she was trying to hear a sound off in the distance. All the while, her eyes kept changing from dark to pale blue.

Suddenly this amazing and peaceful woman seemed to focus on the people surrounding her as she stood and softly spoke.

"I repent, I repent, I repent. I forgive myself for being human and being flawed. I accept God, My Father as my Creator and have a knowing that his son will heal the hearts of the world when it loses the truth again. Hear these words as I am God's Oracle sent to speak His truth. Heed Father's words and you will be made to avoid the darkness that is made up of misery and must surely await you. I will choose to love each of you, with no need of your response as Our Creator has taught. For God's unconditional love is the act of loving each of us without expecting love in return and allowing all to have freewill. It is the truest indication of his love for every one of us. His expectation for your returned love is nothing, although His hope for your returned love is everything."

The crowd around her grew silent as the Oracle spoke. The people of this group seemed unable to look away or interrupt the Oracle's declaration.

The woman then walked to each person in the mob and touched every hand while looking into their eyes. When this woman ended her message for one individual, she would move to the next person. The Oracle would look into their eyes and smile, and speak Father's truth to them, never breaking eye contact until going to the next person.

I realized that when the Oracle would speak for Father, her eyes would change to that pale blue. But when she finished and began making her way to the next person, the color of her eyes would return to dark blue.

That was when I realized Father's attention in the room was on me. He had noticed that I was watching the Oracle's eyes with great curiosity. And seemed amused with my fascination. "My child do not be mystified by the Oracle's eyes glowing. It is only my light and love shining through her eyes. Your eyes have already done the same when speaking my truth." He stated with that same amused smile on his face.

All I could do at that moment was wonder if they had nursing homes in Heaven and if dementia would be the reason Father would check in to the Heavenly Facility.

This amazing woman, this Oracle was willing to take on an entire mob of insanely crazed people and was way cooler than me.

I am sure she is the bravest person that has ever lived. I am very confident that this Oracle didn't even blink when Father asked her, "Do you accept this my child?" No, this woman was already jumping up and clearing her schedule before he finished his question.

The thought ran through my mind that I am not even close to that brave or eloquent with words. My escape plan had changed little since childhood. I still believe you should run away in a zigzag pattern, making it harder to shoot me if my attacker has a gun.

I'm sure I heard Father laugh softly as the zigzag pattern idea came into my head. Oh yeah, He was listening.

When had my eyes done the color changing thing? I silently wondered.

Then I remember, the sweet little old man at the grocery store, in the butter aisle. What had he said when I was running away? "I see the angel in your eyes." I thought he was just being complimentary.

I would find out over the next year that everyone sees something different when God's light and love shine through my eyes.

I had concern at first that people would freak out when the flashlight went on behind my eyes. But most are just fascinated by it.

Some people say they see what they believe to be the gates of Heaven, others say they see Heavenly Father, Mother, or Christ and some see angels. I have learned to be very cautious around young children that get close to my face.

Most of the time children will see angels in my eyes and want to touch them. That zigzag move comes in handy when you have an excited child trying to 'catch' the angel in your eyes. It only took one jab in the eyeball to learn that one.

I realize that Father and Ian are staring at me. *Oh, they are waiting on me* I thought to myself as I turn back to the scene. It seems on pause before me.

The feeling of complete peace that had drawn me to the Oracle now seemed to fall upon the entire cluster of people who had been taunting her previously.

I watched in awe as each person, after hearing the personal message from Father through the Oracle, fell to their knees and began to cry. I could hear the mob now begging the Oracle for her forgiveness and attempting to worship her. The woman now stands in the middle of the crowd.

"Do NOT worship me for I am human just as you! I did not create you, nor this world around you, for that is the work of our Father in Heaven! Your Father that loves you so much he has sent me to share his truth with each of His children so you may live a life of peace, love and joy. A life of peace, love and joy is the absence of fear! I am no better than each of you, just different! I am honored to hear his voice as though he is standing before me! I am not more worthy than any of you to have this gift! It is merely my desire to show each of you that you have the same ears as I! You can hear Our Father, God, as I do!" the Oracle sternly but lovingly shouted to the people.

While I am watching this incredible change from a mob of insane, blood thirsty zombies, to truly repentant loving beings, I realize that the Oracle and the crowd falling at her feet have caught the attention of a group of men. They seem to be unhappy with the turn of events.

I can see the disgust in the men's hard faces as they look at this group of people falling to their knees and begging for forgiveness. I sense that this group of very harsh men see this behavior as weakness. I can feel the anger come over the men as if they are aware this woman, this Oracle of God, has ruined the fear and destruction they had been trying to spread.

The largest and cruelest looking of the men walks toward the crowd, never taking his eyes off the Oracle. He is carrying what appears to be a large sword in his right hand.

The sword looks like they make it from stone and sharpened it on both sides. The hilt of the sword looks as though they wrapped it in fabric.

As this large and cruel man is making his way to the Oracle and her peaceful crowd, the group of men he has just walked away from begin chanting the name Balaam.

I don't know if this man was 'the Balaam' or just named for him but, the sight of him walking toward the crowd was making my stomach churn.

As he approaches God's Oracle, she turns to him as if she knew he was coming and smiles at the monster while he raises his stone sword to detach her head.

"I am ready Father." I hear the Oracle softly say. "I have achieved all that I can for you on this earth. Thank you, Father, for your love and trust in me."

What happened next was horrific and I will not go into the details. But what follows the horror, I will tell you in as much detail as possible. It is vital for you to know the details of that event.

Just as the Oracle was being taken away by Balaam and his cronies, I could hear the crowd of people that had been surrounding the amazing woman whose light was cruelly stomped out. The crowd was sobbing and wailing.

When I looked toward them, I can see that the surrounding area seemed darker somehow without those brilliant blue eyes shining God's light.

The pain and torture I could hear in the voices of the crowd that the Oracle had just saved with God's truth, was almost worse than the pain and suffering I had seen earlier being hurled upon the innocent.

As my mind is trying to take in the chaos before me, everything abruptly goes silent. I look back to where the Oracle's crowd had been but do not see a single soul. They had all just disappeared. Not a single trace, they were just gone.

The other innocent people who were being beating, raped and tortured suddenly disappeared as well. I was so stunned that I almost missed the crazed individuals looking to Balaam in confusion. Unexpectedly, I heard what sounded like thunder. It was so loud that my ears started to ring.

Then it began to rain. This was not your typical rain, but a down pour like nothing I have experienced in all my days. The streets before me began to run red with the blood of the innocent as water began running through the streets like a river.

I see the panic and fear on the faces of the harsh men as they run for cover. The one they called Balaam did not move. He just stood there looking up at the rain with such a look of hate, it made me shudder.

No sooner had I felt the shudder, Balaam looked toward me. I swear we made eye contact as he just stared into my soul. But that was impossible right? This was just a vision.

As he takes a step toward where my husband and I huddle on our bed the vision just blinks out like it was never there.

"Do you comprehend what you just witnessed my children?" Father asked quietly.

"The beginning of the rain you told Noah about. The rain that would flood the earth and the reason you told Noah to build the Ark." my husband said humbly as his voice cracks.

Ian and I were both sobbing and shaking from the sheer volume of knowledge and understanding we had received, and the horrific violence we just witnessed. Seeing what human beings are capable of.

"Father, will I have to die a horrible death like that?" I asked not sure that I truly wanted to know the answer.

Father soothingly replied, "My child, you have much to do. Your Divine Spirit will not relinquish your human body before it is time. Nor would I allow you to suffer."

Basically, He said that I would not die before I am supposed to. All I could think in that moment was that I could sustain a great deal of pain and not die.

Maybe it is time for a new escape plan that involves more than just running fast in a zigzag pattern. I guess it was best that Father showed us this vision after I agreed to the Oracle way of life. I might have broken the whole God protocol of 'needing more time to think about it'.

Suddenly I remembered all the innocent people in the vision that had just disappeared. I did not remember ever reading of that in the bible, not that I have ever been a great scholar of scripture, but I truly feel like I would remember a cool fact like that. Before I could process all the questions forming in my head Father spoke.

"All that had belief in Me and followed the simple rules that are ingrained in your Divine Spirit were ascended into an unanimated state along with all of the beasts of the world. I placed them in the Heavenly realm until it was safe for them to return to earth and their human lives.

Once I returned them to earth, they had no memory of the destruction that was before." Father began speaking in a soft voice and almost hesitant in his words.

He said, "My intent was never to flood the entire earth to the point of complete destruction. My intent was to create enough flooding to destroy the material items that had become more import than humanity to so many. It was my desire that in tragedy, the good in the Divine Spirit would overcome the evil and lies that society had spread across the earth. That my children would treasure love above greed. That they would choose kindness and banish cruelty. Then my precious daughter, my Oracle was murdered, and her body paraded through the streets. I do take responsibility for the choices I made that day. My promise to all my future children was the gift of the rainbow. The rainbow is made from the essence of love and my promise to never flood the entire earth again."

It was at that moment I had the most insane thought and I instantly felt ashamed. Before I could say anything, Father spoke.

"It is always a difficult day to find out your parents are NOT perfect." He said lovingly and with humor in his voice.

As if reading my mind, which He was, Father continued with, "I am not perfect in ACTION my child, rather I have perfect KNOWLEDGE. I also have perfect FORGIVENESS and LOVE for ALL my children."

"If Heaven and I were perfect in all sense, why would there have been need of the war of the angels? If Heaven and I were perfect, your brother Lucifer would have never fallen." Father said with a look that told me I had so much more to learn.

Father had been speaking to Ian and me for an hour at this point.

We did not know that we still had two more hours to go.

THE END, FOR NOW

To see Ian's bird designs, check out www.authorgodsoracle.com

Love Eternal, God's Oracle

Made in the USA
Middletown, DE
28 July 2024